UNLEASH YOUR PRIMAL BRAIN

Praise for

Unleash Your Primal Brain

"In highly readable style, Tim Ash moves readers from the basics of brain functioning to the evolution of its regularities, quirks, and affordances. In the process, we gain **invaluable insights into human decision-making and behavior.**"

Robert Cialdini—*New York Times* bestselling author of *Influence* and *Pre-Suasion*

"**A fascinating and thrilling look into our minds and what matters.**"

Jay Baer—Founder of Convince & Convert, co-author of *Talk Triggers*

"Tim has studied the research on behavioral science and evolutionary psychology and written an excellent book that explains much of human behavior. **If you want to know why we do what we do, then read this book.**"

Susan Weinschenk, PhD—Author of *100 Things Every Designer Needs to Know About People*

"This book would be very helpful for anyone who wants to understand what truly drives attention, emotions and cognitive arousal, from the perspective of psychology! **Very addictive read by an author with great experience and academic knowledge.** I highly recommend this book!"

Dr. Hedda Martina Šola—Dir. of the Institute for Neuromarketing, Oxford Business College

"A no-nonsense look at what drives us—**exposes the evolutionary "why" behind our actions!**"

Phil Barden—Managing Director of DECODE, bestselling author of *Decoded: The science behind why we buy*

"Managing your brain is the job of your life. This book is **a good way to understand the operating system we've inherited.**"

Loretta Breuning, PhD—Author of *Habits of a Happy Brain*

"Before you try to change someone's mind or convince somebody to buy from you, it would be wise to understand how that spongy thing in our skull works. From chemistry and biology to psychology and evolution, Tim Ash cracks open the skull (almost literally) to uncover and explain the magic of it all. Unleash Your Primal Brain is a journey and a directive. **When you can better understand how we think, you will be primed to know how to make others take action.** As much as things have changed, Tim brings it all back to basics… this is one primal read…"

Mitch Joel—Author, *Six Pixels of Separation* and *CTRL ALT Delete*

"They say the mind has a mind of its own. In this **fantastic book**, Tim introduces us to a strange, wild, but somehow exceedingly familiar friend—our own brain."

Robert Rose—Keynote speaker, content strategist, bestselling author of *Killing Marketing*

"**What a wild ride!** Tim's ambitious book takes us from early life on earth, to the bizarre qualities that make us uniquely human. Sleep, memory, herd instinct, motivation, language, culture, cooperation—it's all in there. **A must-read book that will literally blow your mind!**"

Joel Comm—*New York Times* bestselling author, keynote speaker, futurist

"A provocative primer on our primal selves! **A must-read to understand why our behavior can create both failures and massive wins.**"

AmyK Hutchens—Award-winning speaker & bestselling author of *GET IT: Five Steps to the Sex, Salary and Success You Want*

"Tim has a deep passion for making the complexities of human behavior fun, fast and easy to understand. **If you want to understand human behavior, this should be on your nightstand.** Don't overthink this decision—go with your primal brain and be blown away!"

Will Leach—Author of *Marketing to Mindstates*

"Learn what it means to be truly human—our evolution comes alive in Tim's vivid book about the most fascinating art and science of our primal selves. **A treasure-trove of unexpected insights!**"

Bryan Kramer—Keynote, CEO of H2H Companies, bestselling author of *Human to Human* and *Shareology*

"**A compelling and highly readable tour de force** that will help many people become better versions of themselves by answering the age-old question of why we do the things we do."

Lance Loveday—CEO, Closed Loop, Author of *Average Is Losing*

"Buckle up: Tim Ash lets you ride shotgun through the nooks, crannies, and hidden valleys of your own mind. **An epic, fun joyride!**"

Ann Handley—Keynote speaker, *Wall Street Journal* bestselling author of *Everybody Writes* and *Content Rules*

"Tim Ash explains how to **reliably persuade others from the inside out** in his exciting new book."

Nir Eyal—*New York Times* bestselling author of *Hooked* and *Indistractable*

UNLEASH YOUR PRIMAL BRAIN

Demystifying how we think and why we act

TIM ASH

ISBN 9781925995299

Published in Australia and New Zealand by

Booktopia Editions, an imprint of Booktopia Pty Ltd

Unit E1, 3-29 Birnie Avenue, Lidcombe, NSW 2141, Australia

For additional information about the author, please visit **TimAsh.com** and **PrimalBrain.com**

Cover & Graphics Design: Dale Shimato

Editing: Christine LePorte

Printed and bound in Australia by Ligare

The paper this book is printed on is in accordance with the standards of the Forest Stewardship Council®. The FSC® promotes environmentally responsible, socially beneficial and economically viable management of the world's forests.

booktopia.com.au

To my parents Tanya and Alexander,
who sacrificed so very much to create
a wondrous and unexpected life for me.

To my brother Artem,
who lives with an open heart and wisdom.

To my wife Britt,
without whose love and support I could
not carry on the sacred work of family.

To my children Alexander and Anya,
who teach me to be better every day and
for whom I strive to build a better world.

I love you all!

TABLE OF CONTENTS

ACKNOWLEDGEMENTS

This is my third book, and I have come to realize that writing one is not a discrete process. It does not begin with the first words in a notebook, nor end on a printed page. The ideas have been circulating inside of me, and have been shared and refined with others for many years. Echoes of the published book will continue to intertwine with my life far in the future.

Endless love and gratitude to my wife Britt, and children Alex and Anya. The countless hours that I spent writing this book were hours that I could not spend with you. That is my great loss.

Much love and respect to Marty Greif, Robyn Benensohn, Dale Shimato, Erik Itzkowitz, Snejana Norris, Alexander Svensson, and the rest of the SiteTuners team—you helped to validate and apply much of the powerful neuromarketing principles that I cover in this book in order to create massive value for our online marketing clients.

I want to thank Mark Levy of LevyInnovation.com for brilliant and powerful conversations to define, sharpen, and position this book. I am grateful to the many friends and colleagues in the online marketing industry for their feedback, caring, and support over the years: Ada Pally, Adam Kahn, Alan K'Necht, Allan Dick, Alex Langshur, Alexandra Watkins, Alice

Kuepper, Alison Harris, Allison Hartsoe, Alyse Speyer, Amy Landino, AmyK Hutchens, Andrew Beckman, Andrew Goodman, Andy Crestodina, Ann Handley, Anne F. Kennedy, Arnie Kuenn, Barbara Koll, Bart Schutz, Bill Hunt, Bill Leake, BJ Fogg, Bjorn Espenes, Brad Geddes, Brant Cooper, Brian Halligan, Brian Massey, Brian Schulman, Bryan Kramer, Bryan Eisenberg, Byron White, Charlie Cole, Charlotte Del Signore, Chuck Mullins, Corey Koberg, Dan Holsenback, Dan Mcgaw, Dana Todd, David Rodnitzky, David Szetela, Dharmesh Shaw, Don Norman, Eileen Hahn, Elizabeth Hannan, Elyse Kaye, Eric Enge, Eric Qualman, Geno Prussakov, Gianpaolo Lorusso, Glenn Mersereau, Glenn Millar, Greg White, Hansen Hunt, Hedda Martina Šola, Hunter Boyle, Jamie Smith, Jacco vanderKooij, Janet Driscoll-Miller, Jay Baer, Jeffrey Eisenberg, Jenny Evans, Jessica Ann, Jim Kukral, Jim Banks, Jim Sterne, Jodi Gaines, Joe Besdin, Joe Pulizzi, Joe Megibow, Joel Comm, Joel Harvey, John Hossack, John Marshall, John Whalen, Justin Rondeau, Kate O'Neill, Katrin Queck, Kelly Peters, Kevin Lee, Khalid Saleh, Krista Neher, Lance Loveday, Larry Kim, Larry Marine, Lars Helgeson, Leanne Webb, Lee Mills, Lee Odden, Lena Fussan, Loretta Breuning, Lou Weiss, Marc Poirer, Mark Jackson, Mark Knowles, Mark Plutowski, Marty Weintraub, Maryna Hradovich, Matt Bailey, Matt McGowan, Matthew Finlay, Maura Ginty, Melanie Mitchell, Michael Bonfils, Michael Stebbins, Michele Baker, Mike Roberts, Mitch Joel, Mo Gawdat, Mona Patel, Nancy Harhut, Natalie Henley, Nir Eyal, Patrick Bultema, Peep Laja, Peter Leifer II, Phil Barden, Phil Leahy, Rich Page, Rick Perreault, Rob Snell, Robert Rose, Robert Cialdini, Roger Dooley, Roland Frasier, Ruth Carter, Sandra Finlay, Sandra Niehaus, Scott Brinker, Sean Ellis, Seth Godin, Shawn Elledge, Shirley Tan, Stas Gromin, Stephan Bajajo, Steve Biafore, Steve Krug, Stewart Quealy, Sujan Patel, Susan Weinschenk, Ted Roxbury, Thad Kahlow, Tobias Queck, Todd Crawford, Ton Wesseling, Tony Nash, Warren Jolly, Will Leach, Willem Knibbe, Valentin Radu, and Vasil Azarov.

If I have inadvertently forgotten anyone, please forgive me and blame the publishing deadline.

WHY YOU SHOULD READ THIS BOOK

This is the story of what makes us human.

Our ancient and most recent evolution created our psychology. We are not rational, logical robots. Nor are we simply wild beasts. Rather, we are a powerful mix of the two. I want to paint a vivid picture of how we became such an odd species.

Yet, there is no way to capture this completely. I will be the first to admit that the evolutionary perspective is only one of many. A beautiful alchemy makes us unique. We cannot reduce that simply to our physical beings.

Even though this book is about the brain, I hope you will bring your heart to it.

It is only the heart that truly sees—inward to our deepest needs, and outward towards connection and unity with the greater universe. I invite you to open your whole being and experience humankind through the eyes of wisdom.

"For me there is only the traveling on paths that have heart, on any path that may have heart, and the only worthwhile challenge is to traverse its full length–and there I travel looking, looking breathlessly."

—Carlos Castaneda, The Teachings of Don Juan: A Yaqui Way of Knowledge

Welcome to the human race

My goal is ambitious—to explain what makes us human from the perspective of evolution.

We share the roots of our brains and behaviors with our ancient cousins. But our very recent evolution has taken us on a path different from our great-ape relatives. Our newfound abilities are stunning—but still rest on the foundations of earlier evolutionary machinery.

Learn to embrace the messy reality of your amazing brain. Think of it as a crash course—Being Human 101. The scope is massive, yet I made the book readable and accessible to a broad audience.

The book I wanted did not exist

I read a lot—dozens of books every year.

Books provide windows into the minds and ideas of others. They are like razor-sharp swords. They cut away ignorance, open new vistas and paths, and fire up my passions and imagination.

People have explored the depths of the ocean and the vast expanse of our cosmos. I believe that the brain is the last unexplored frontier. The very fact that we can use our brains to study our brains is a stunning self-referential feat of magic!

I have searched through hundreds of books, articles, scientific papers, and videos. Yet nothing painted the picture that was growing in my mind.

Experts stayed within their isolated silos, and did not collaborate to connect to a larger picture. Editors summarized key results, but in their descriptions of the "what" and the "how" they often neglected the underlying "why."

Like the story of Goldilocks and the three bears, none of it was "just right" for me. It was either too detailed, too broad, too disconnected, or only applicable to specific groups of people and not all of humanity.

So, I decided to write my own book

But I was not starting from zero.

My undergraduate and Ph.D. work was in computer engineering, cognitive science, and neural networks. I studied self-organizing computer systems which learn from repeated examples. This field is now called Artificial Intelligence. I was lucky enough to study at the University of California, San Diego. UCSD is a world-class institution whose reputation continues to climb like a rocket a mere half century since its founding. There, I had the privilege to study in an interdisciplinary intellectual stew. Neuroscientists, economists, user experience pioneers, psychologists, computer scientists, and linguists all collaborated. The experience taught me to cut across boundaries and synthesize diverse information.

I must confess—I am a quitter.

I never finished my Ph.D. After seven years of graduate school, I launched my first business instead. This was during the early birth of the Internet age, and I ran a digital agency to help launch new startups. My focus shifted to making websites more effective. This field is known by the longwinded label of Conversion Rate Optimization (CRO). CRO is cross-disciplinary and encompasses psychology, user experience, copywriting, web design, and split-testing. For twenty years, our crack staff at SiteTuners worked with top companies and nimble startups around the globe. We created over $1,200,000,000 in value for clients including Google, Cisco, Expedia, Nespresso, Siemens, Thomson Reuters, and Intuit.

Along the way, I wrote two bestselling books on Landing Page Optimization. The second, much-improved, edition resulted from the massive help of my uber-smart colleagues Maura Ginty and Rich Page.

I also founded and for ten years chaired the international Conversion Conference event series, with events in the US, UK, Germany, and France. It was exciting to help grow a new digital marketing discipline!

About my writing process

When I sat down to write, I first had to start by reading.

I reread over thirty books, as well as countless articles, blog posts, and scientific papers. From these, I shaped my vision of evolution and psychology. I have listed all the books in the Appendix. I want to inspire you to read some of them because I have kindled your excitement about a particular subject. Many of the books described the same observations from different perspectives. I removed redundancies, thought deeply about key evolutionary implications, and threw away interesting but extraneous details which did not support the main narrative of my story.

Then the real work began.

I created and massaged the book outline and chapter headings. Then I took all of the material and rearranged it into my unique story arc. I added my ideas, frameworks, and thought experiments at this stage. Then I wrote and considered every word. I hope that you will hear my vivid and dynamic voice throughout the whole book.

This book is not for you if...

Every book is not for every possible reader. This book is no exception.

Let me save you some time with a quick checklist of who should NOT read this book:

- **I want annotations and footnotes to interrupt my reading**—I do not want to break up the flow or readability of this book, and want you to focus on the concepts themselves. You live a busy life and I am trying to give you the important stuff in a straight read of the text. The point is not to turn this into a research project, or worse yet, a book that you will abandon. Feel free to read the sourcebooks in the Appendix if you want more details.

- **I want specific scientific studies to support what you are saying**—Any study that I cite will only apply narrowly to its particular circumstances, and may soon be superseded by newer findings. In any case, if you were to apply it to your specific situation, your results would vary. I want you to understand the biases, shortcuts, and tendencies we all share, and the fact that they exist.
- **I want simple superficial concepts and dumbed-down language**—This book is for the person who wants to stretch, learn, and grow. I provide as much detail and nuance as possible. I have done my best to make the language vivid, and to explain the concepts clearly. The readers of this book are smart, and I refuse to pander to the lowest common denominator in the hopes of growing the audience.
- **I want this book to apply to my professional field**—This book is already stuffed to the rafters explaining *why* our brains came to be. The application of it to a particular field would require a separate book on each subject. But stay tuned in the future and you might get your wish…

This book is for you!

This book is designed to be a lively read. I hope to take you through fascinating terrain as your guide, and I know you are up for this exploration!

My purpose is to provide the unified and cohesive "why" behind our behavior—to connect the dots among seemingly disparate perspectives on the workings of the brain.

Much of what you will learn can apply to a variety of activities. If I tried to cover possible applications in this book, it would become a jumbled hodgepodge. However, you can mine it repeatedly for insights into your personal and professional life. Reread with fresh eyes to find ties to personal development, marketing, sales, leadership, community building, politics, management, addiction, intimate relationships, and many other areas.

If you've made it this far, this book is for you—let's Unleash Your Primal Brain!

INTRODUCTION

It's dessert time!

There is a juicy apple in front of you, and a slice of chocolate cake.

You are free to choose.

Or are you?

The choice was made for you—hundreds of millions of years ago!

This book is about the commonalities all 8,000,000,000 people on earth share.

Our ancestors were molded by ruthless survival pressures from the earliest days of life on the planet. Adaptations which worked long ago are still inside of us—also shared with insects and reptiles. Later additions are common to all mammals from the tiniest shrews to the most massive whales. Some capabilities were bolted on relatively recently, and are only shared with our primate cousins. And the runaway explosion of humans on the planet can only be explained by our bizarre species-level evolution.

> The only way to understand how our brains work is to examine the complete evolutionary arc.

I don't care if you are young or old, rich or poor, introverted or extroverted. It is not about our individual differences. This book describes the basic operating system of how we all deal with life.

Drop a rock. It falls and hits the ground.

Once you understand brain evolution, many of our behaviors will become more predictable. To a scary degree, we are reactive animals ruled by passions, and not the rational geniuses with free will that we like to imagine.

First the bad news: The notion that people make decisions and choices to maximize objective self-interest has been demolished. People are not rational—far from it.

Now the good news: We are finding out exactly how and why we act in these seemingly irrational ways. In other words, there is a method to our madness.

My view of the brain is heavily influenced by evolutionary biology and psychology. I don't believe we have arrived at a perfect brain design, or that humankind deserves an exalted and special place in the universe. Rather, we are a band of super-cooperative apes who have come to dominate the planet. In the process we have wiped out whole ecosystems in our voracious destructiveness. At this moment we are by far the most dominant force shaping the very destiny of life on earth.

We evolved for a particular environment, but our rapid social advances and mushrooming populations have created a bewildering new world. On the timescale of this dizzying change, evolution has effectively stopped, and we must rely on what has gotten us this far. By retracing the path that our distant ancestors took to get here, we can understand the stunning abilities and glaring weaknesses which we have inherited.

Sometimes our reactions and responses are appropriate and uncannily helpful. In the blink of an eye we can assess complex situations and reach critical life-or-death decisions. At other times, we are seemingly our own worst enemies—repeating the same mistakes, even when we know the results will be counterproductive, or even deadly.

Unlocking the true nature of the human brain is the last frontier. Recent work in fields such as biology, neuroscience, evolutionary psychology, medical imaging, social science, and behavioral economics is combining to show us the inner workings of this evolutionary marvel.

This book is designed for you—the curious and intelligent searcher for truth.

I want to give you the essentials, and draw you a map of the wondrous terrain inside of the human mind.

You will forever be altered by the journey we are about to undertake together. It may seem like an alien landscape at first. But you will gain valuable perspectives which will allow you to live your life with a new appreciation of what makes us tick.

Forget the advanced technology all around you—let's explore inside of the bony skull which guards the treasures within…

Get ready, it's going to be a wild ride!

PART I

FOUNDATIONS

Chapter 1
THE LIE OF RATIONALITY

The big lie

We have been sold a lie. And it's a big one.

It has been circulating in various forms for thousands of years. It warps our view of ourselves, other people, and our very relationship to the world around us. The lie has far-reaching implications, and is insidious because we desperately want to believe it.

We are special primarily because of our capacity for rational thought, unlike wild animals.

Reasoning, discourse, objectivity, truth, rationality, delayed gratification, and planning—all bound up into one giant belief about our basic nature. "I think, therefore I exist," declared Descartes three and a half centuries ago. We are all his philosophical grandchildren.

Consider the alternative—no one wants to be irrational, hotheaded, random, or unpredictable. A society based on such people could not function and civilization would devolve into chaos and violence.

Worse yet, we are certainly not lumbering beasts lashing out from reflex, or ruled by strong emotions and passions. None of us want to believe we are fickle, weak, or easy to manipulate.

Even if our emotions sometimes overpower us, we believe the rational part of our brain is at least in control most of the time. It is the benevolent and calm overlord and master.

The big lie is very flattering and feels good—we are different not in *degree*, but rather in *kind* from other animals. We are special!

Emotions and decisions

Emotions are considered an annoying artifact of our primitive selves. We feel we would make much better choices were it not for the distorting effects of strong passions. In fact, we have it backward.

Without emotions we are paralyzed. Our conscious brain can analyze information and present us with options. But it is powerless to decide.

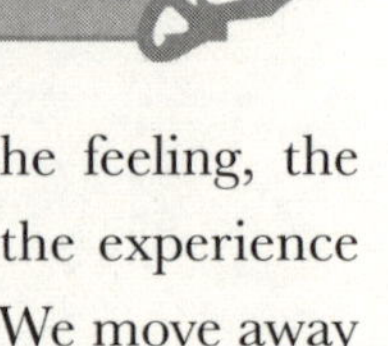

Emotions are the guideposts for survival. The stronger the feeling, the more immediately we must react to it. We move towards the experience of positive emotions, expecting something good to happen. We move away from the experience of negative ones, hoping to avoid pain.

Our emotions are a snapshot of all information available to the primal brain. Our "gut" feeling is generally reliable, and helps us to choose among available options. Emotions are based on chemical helpers which evolved to deal with survival challenges in the distant past across a wide array of species.

But emotions are not foolproof. Shortcuts and automatic instincts helped our ancestors to survive. But our distant past is unlike the "civilized" world in which we find ourselves. Many of the responses that got our ancestors here are often suboptimal and counterproductive in modern societies. Unfortunately, there is not much we can do about it.

Evolution has effectively stopped and we are no longer in the natural world. But we are still forced to use the brains which developed to deal with it.

Why do we fight so hard against this emotion-driven view of our brains?

There is another untold part of the story—our conscious mind wants to make meaning out of the world around it. In a chaotic environment, it looks for hints and patterns to help it predict the future. We tell ourselves stories involving cause and effect. These stories are nothing more than an alibi and a cover-up.

With modern brain imaging techniques, we can see decisions made in the primal brain. Only after a significant delay do portions of the conscious mind wake up, to justify or verbally describe them.

Every decision is made long before our awareness can fabricate a retrospective "reason" for it.

Science fiction great Robert Heinlein was speaking about all humankind when he declared, "Man is not a rational animal; he is a rationalizing animal."

We can try to understand ourselves consciously, through dialogue, therapy, or mindfulness practices. But we will never have direct access to the older parts of the brain. Through brutal competition and evolutionary pressures, they have gotten our ancestors through the first billion years of life on this planet. Those primordial and wordless depths are the origin of most of our actions and decisions.

It would be too cumbersome and slow if we were to deliberately use the modern parts of the brain for everything. In the animal world there are the quick and the dead, and rest assured that your ancestors were all quick, or you would not be here.

The primal parts of the brain are still there—working tirelessly, with massive capacity and lightning speed. They are well suited to make most decisions and initiate appropriate actions. The modern, energy-intensive parts of the brain are kept largely deactivated. They are only woken when their special abilities would be complementary and useful to the primal brain for the task at hand.

We are the products of evolution

The notion of humankind's special place in the universe keeps getting pushed further into a corner by the advances of science.

We no longer live under the notion that the whole universe revolves around the earth in a mechanical celestial dance. We know that we are on a planet that orbits an insignificant star. The star is on the outer edge of an unremarkable galaxy, which itself is one of at least two hundred billion others. Our sun has 700,000,000,000,000,000,000,000,000,000,000,000,000 (700 trillion septillion) sisters. Planets, including ones that can sustain life, orbit many of those.

Evolution has produced countless species throughout billions of years on earth. To think people are somehow apart from this process is the height of arrogance, or intentional willful ignorance. We are all connected to the very first self-replicating virus—the mother of us all.

Chance and circumstance

We are dandelion seeds blowing in the wind.

Even the subtlest of initial nudges can set us on radically divergent paths which we cannot foresee. Sensory inputs bombard us completely unnoticed, while shaping us profoundly.

Our current state—the sum total of what has brought us to this moment, and the memories encoded in it—also influences us. For example, a person scarred by war or personal trauma in early life is forever wired differently. Even subtle forces will guarantee that we respond to the same events unlike others. Some of these influences can be recent—mere hours, minutes, or seconds before. Most people would, for example, agree that they react more impulsively when they are sleep-deprived or hungry.

The machinery of our primal brain automatically examines, prioritizes, and ignores the vast majority of the information it receives. If necessary, it occasionally acts as well—enhancing our survival prospects from moment to moment.

We are at the mercy of powerful forces that we cannot comprehend, or even see. Both inside and outside of our bodies, we are not really in control. The notion that we are the masters of our life destiny, or the active "choosers" of our decisions, is nothing more than a comforting illusion.

Chapter 2

THE BIG PICTURE OF BRAIN EVOLUTION

Life without brains

The Big Bang!

Thirteen point eight billion years ago our universe blinked into existence, and started to fly apart. Matter eventually began to coalesce—forming stars. Nuclear furnaces ignited, enabling fusion. Lighter elements transformed within the hearts of stars into heavier ones. Dust clouds compacted under their gravitational pull and formed solid clumps or gaseous spheres. Some got captured by the pull of nearby stars.

Our earth formed 4.6 billion years ago. Almost immediately life took hold. It may have emerged under liquid oceans and near volcanic hydrothermal vents as early as 4.28 billion years ago. But it was definitely established by the 3.48-billion-year mark in many other places.

The prerequisites for life are clear. It must be able to reproduce and propagate itself. This can happen by direct copying or cloning, or by more elaborate means. The reproduction must happen consistently and accurately—with viable organisms reliably resulting. This *copying fidelity* is important. Otherwise repeated copying mistakes would doom survival across many generations. Life must also be fruitful, and reproduce often enough to ensure that the species does not die out. The exact level of *fecundity* depends on how harsh or welcoming the environment happens to be. This is a tough balance. During hard times having a few extra offspring might be an insurance policy. But it could just as easily be a waste of energy which dims your survival prospects.

Note what is not on the list of requirements for life—a brain. Indeed, early lifeforms did not have brains at all.

Why do we need a brain?

The first solid evidence we have of a brain is only 520 million years old. There is a very long gap between the emergence of life and the emergence of brains.

So, why do we need one?

There are plenty of lifeforms on earth that function without a brain at all, and they are doing just fine. Look around (with a microscope) at the fungi, microbes, bacteria, and viruses. You are swimming in an invisible soupy cloud of them right now. None of them have a brain, yet are very effective at being alive.

Of course, those are relatively simple creatures. They are not even composed of cells. A cell is a miniature wonder. It contains a powerplant, garbage disposal, invasion defense force, factories, and maintenance facilities.

What if we were to consider multicellular life?

We live on a planet covered by complex multicellular plants of various kinds. Plants exhibit many adaptive behaviors that can seem intelligent. Flowers open only when the sun comes out. Sap heals and repairs wounds. Eucalyptus trees poison nearby competitors by shedding toxic bark. Certain pine seeds only germinate after the heat of a forest fire—sprouting when there is an opportunity to thrive. But none of this requires a brain.

What if we looked only at animals?

Another seeming dead end. There are whole subdivisions of animal life which also function just fine without a brain. These include sea urchins, corals, jellyfish, and starfish. Such marine creatures thrived well before any of our ancestors slithered onto dry land.

There is even evidence that brains once existed and were later jettisoned among animals. Certain sponges are descended from creatures that had brains. But the cost of maintaining a brain is high. So, among these sponges, brains just evolved away.

The humble sea squirt gives us a key clue to the reason that brains exist. This marine animal is born with a brain and the ability to swim. It sets off and finds a nice rock where it attaches itself for the rest of its life. What happens next is truly bizarre. It eats its own brain! That's right, it uses the energy from dissolving its brain to build a digestive system instead. Once it is attached to its permanent home, it gets nutrients from food that floats by. The brain is no longer needed and its energy content is recycled.

The brain evolved to respond to rapid changes in a world requiring movement.

Following the recipe

"Ontogeny recapitulates phylogeny"—a mouthful of Greek, but the concept is important. Ontogeny is the physical development of an organism. Phylogeny means that to grow, it goes through all the important intermediate forms of its ancestors throughout evolution.

Think of all life as a basic genetic recipe. You can tweak it and make refinements, or even add steps. But you must still follow the proper order to build. In the womb we all go through the stages of cellular division and differentiation. Then we add a heartbeat and circulatory system, and grow tadpole limbs. Afterward, we build eyes and a brain, and suppress the growth of the tail at the end of the spine. Eventually, we morph our pig-like bodies into something resembling a human. Billions of years of evolution replays on fast-forward to create us!

This is also true of brain development. The ancient brainstem and motor cortex develop first. The frontal lobes are not mature until the end of our young adult years. The prefrontal cortex is the last area to come fully online in people—only in their mid-twenties! This is the part that governs planning, self-control, and "executive function."

In humans, the brain is especially flexible during youth, when it makes great leaps in size and ability. It is capable of continual adaptations in later life as well. The brain can magically remap sensors and muscle control after some severe physical injuries, and adapt to its new reality. It also gets smarter by growing new brain cells in the presence of short-term fasting and hunger, to increase the chances of finding food in the future. Yet the basic idea of following our genetic recipe to build it in the first place is critical.

Evolution kept what worked, then added new brain capabilities which helped us to adapt and survive.

Key brain systems

Before I get torn to pieces by an angry pack of neuroscientists and paleontologists, I must admit this is all very much oversimplified. The real brain is more complicated. But I am still going to sketch the simple outlines of it.

Think of the human brain as organized into four systems. Each of these has discrete subsystems. Many of them are richly interconnected, and interact by passing information to each other. Sometimes they cooperate. Sometimes they compete with, or even override, each other.

I will occasionally mention specific brain areas and chemicals throughout the book. But you do not have to memorize or master these details.

The four main systems of the human brain are:

- **Basic survival**—Keeping the lights on is the responsibility of the *brainstem* and *hypothalamus*. This is what keeps your heart beating when you are asleep, and makes sure that you keep breathing even when you are unconscious.
- **Complex automatic responses**—The limbic system encompasses the *amygdala, hippocampus, cingulate gyrus, thalamus*, and *the septal area*. It is in charge of memories, emotions, and arousal. These areas are all related because strong emotions and stimulation create the most vivid memories. Memories help us to survive when we encounter similar circumstances in the future.
- **Conscious movement and actions**—The *basal ganglia* are critical for conscious movement and control of our body. They allows us to learn new motor skills and optimizes them over time by repetition and experience.
- **Social behavior and planning**—The *prefrontal cortex* handles much of what makes us the most social mammals on the planet. We can effectively cooperate in vast networks of millions of strangers. This allows us to carry out incredibly complex plans of staggering

duration. It also enables a fluid understanding of our place in the social tribe. We can reason about various courses of action by simulating and modeling them internally.

It would be wrong to call the above "layers" since they do not operate separately from each other. There are strong direct connections among them. For example, the orbitofrontal cortex (OFC) is the part of the brain that unifies strong emotions. We can then incorporate them into our conscious decision-making process. To accomplish this, the OFC connects directly into the brainstem, as well as the amygdala. By communicating this way, it ties decision-making to basic survival and the experience of fear in more ancient brain structures.

Keep the following basics in mind:

- Our brain retained and tweaked ancient brain structures which continued to be useful. All major systems have existed for a long time across many species because the basic design proved useful. But their arrangement, complexity, and size vary widely.
- Compared to older species, the newer areas of human brains are much more developed. They are also richly interconnected with the ancient parts.
- The dominant brain system active at a given point depends on the circumstances. During times of danger our ancient survival instincts override the modern brain structures. The social thinking areas operate only when there are no immediate threats.

Simplifying to make it useful

Having barely scratched the surface of the true complexity of the brain, I am going to simplify even further. I want to break the brain into two parts relevant for our purposes:

- **The primal brain**—The primal brain is a combination of all ancient structures which handle most of your life on autopilot. It is focused on survival imperatives. The primal brain processes massive amounts of information, works non-stop, and never gets tired. It combines widely disparate information into instant decisions and actions. We sometimes experience this embodied intelligence as an intuition or a "gut feeling." To do its work quickly, the primal brain takes shortcuts. It relies on automatic impulses and taps instincts learned from past experiences.

  The primal brain responds to arousal, as well as to positive and negative emotions. Most situations which do not elicit a strong reaction are ruthlessly ignored. Ignoring and simplifying has dual advantages—conserving energy and speeding up decisions.
- **The conscious brain**—The more modern parts of the brain are the ones we can access through conscious thought and awareness. These include areas for planning and mapping out the ever-shifting dynamics of our place in the social tribe. This part of the brain is also responsible for language and abstract symbolic thought.

  The conscious brain requires massive energy, has very limited capacity, and tires quickly. It can also be easily distracted or waylaid. The conscious brain thinks it is in charge. It is actually mostly kept on standby by the hardworking primal brain. The conscious brain is only consulted when there are no immediate survival threats and a novel situation arises. When not engaged in abstract thought, it defaults to thinking exclusively about the social sphere.

The cooperation and tug-of-war between these two brains are at the heart of this book.

Chapter 3
BRAIN BASICS

Gross anatomy

Philosophical debates about consciousness aside, I will refer to the brain, versus the mind, throughout this book. The tendency is to think of the brain as separate from the rest of the body—a control unit and a master, which acts as a puppeteer which compels the body to do things.

The brain is not only the jelly-like contents inside of our skulls. A more accurate view would be to consider the whole central nervous system. Besides the brain, it has tentacles running as a thick cord through the spine, and connects to the farthest reaches of the body. These peripheral nerves are inside of every muscle, organ, and joint. They extend to the very tips of your fingers and toes.

The brain can act through nerve cells very quickly on all parts of the body. The *autonomic* (visceral) nervous system is wired directly to the evolutionarily oldest parts of the brain. It supports the functioning of respiration, digestion, sleep, and other subconscious processes. The *musculoskeletal* (voluntary) nervous system allows us to consciously move our body and is wired into motor control areas of various evolutionary ages.

Signals from the body pass to the brain via the *axons* of the nerve cells. These thin wire-like structures can extend up to one meter in length. Insulating fat protects axons to prevent cross-talk and noise from surrounding activities. Think of the axons as the electrical cables of the body—transmitting information quickly and reliably over great distances.

These signals travel together either through the spinal cord or directly into the brain stem. From there, they are passed along to many connected regions within the brain.

But neurons don't directly touch other neurons. To form a chain and transmit information, they have to bridge small gaps between each other. These spaces are called *synapses*, and have their own complicated anatomy. Action at the synapses slows down to chemical speeds. Each axon squirts a specialized compound called a *neurotransmitter*. Some nearby neurons have areas that are designed to detect and capture molecules of that particular chemical. These receptors are tuned to only "listen" to specific neurotransmitters as they float across the synapse. On the other side of the gap, neurotransmitters bind to the matching receptors. Once this binding happens, the neuron passes on the information electrically via its axons to other neurons.

The brain is a well-protected organ. It's not only shielded by a heavy bone skull, but also buffered from physical shocks with fluid. It operates in a very temperature-controlled environment. Even a tenth of a degree temperature change can fry its delicate functions. Several degrees Celsius of fever can be tolerated by the body, but once the brain fails to maintain an even temperature, the game is over. Massive amounts of blood needed to support the brain must be filtered through the blood-brain barrier. This prevents harmful chemical compounds from polluting the delicate environment inside.

Despite all this protection, certain chemicals can reach the brain via the bloodstream and influence it. These are produced naturally inside the body, or can be introduced from the outside. The brain can also produce signaling chemicals which get sent to the body, or direct their manufacture within other organs.

The brain is not the body's puppet master. There is a constant two-way electrical and chemical dialogue between the brain and the rest of the body.

The brain itself is not a monolithic unit. Some imagine it as a tangled bowl of spaghetti, in which every part is massively and randomly connected to every other part. Somehow out of this mess thought and action supposedly emerge. In reality, most connections in the brain are fairly local and communicate with nearby areas. When there are longer connections to farther brain regions, they are relatively sparse. In other words, the brain has its own internal organization, and is best viewed as a system of different areas or regions with specific functions.

Experience wires the brain

Some parts of our brain follow a set of automatic routines as determined by our genes, and are not designed for learning. We need such innate knowledge to control digestion, respiration, metabolism, biorhythms, and circulation. We also need effective and immediate responses in cases of fight-or-flight emergencies. None of these involve learning.

Portions of human brains learn from experience. This allows us to become better adapted to the specific environment in which we will live.

Much of this learning happens when we are young children, as we interact with other people and our environment. It is very hard to override these early learnings consciously as an adult. You can think of early childhood as a second wave of environment-specific instincts that develop for each of us individually.

Our brains change very dramatically during early childhood and are extremely flexible. At a certain stage, parts of our brains explode into a wild tangle of new connections—wiring neurons to as many possible neighbors as they can. As early as ages two to seven, we prune this bushy thicket back to something much more manageable. Children take in vast amounts of experience and start to organize them into a personal view of "the way things are." Each of us have different experiences from the moment of birth, and even in the womb. Our resulting instincts will be unique when combined with the influence of our genes. In a very real sense, these early life experiences become our reality, and our truth.

Why does this rapid over-connection stage happen? At first, we don't know what is important. But eventually the connections between two neurons which fire at the same time will get stronger. They are reinforced neurochemically and structurally. Connections are surrounded by a thicker layer of insulating fat. The result is better signal transmission—without cross-talk or noise from other nearby neurons. This process makes it easier for the neurons to work in tandem in the future.

Our brains automatically build associations between events that repeatedly occur at the same time, or in the same place. If something happens once, it may just be random. But if it happens regularly, we will learn the pattern of it.

What fires together wires together.

Experience makes order out of the initial chaos. Connections which co-occur happen more easily. Alternatives that are not commonly used fade away through neglect. Over time some associations become as easy to execute as speeding down an empty highway in a sports car. Others continue to require massive effort, akin to trekking on foot through the wilderness—every step a conscious labor.

Use it or lose it

Once the major growth phases are over, our adult brains are still capable of change. If you lose a finger due to an accident, the sensory processing areas of the brain can be remapped to nearby parts of the body. New brain cells also grow as a result of short- and long-term fasting.

The strengthening of connections between neurons is largely driven by emotion and repetition. If something is experienced as emotionally positive, we will want to repeat it. If it is emotionally negative, we will try to avoid it.

Strong emotions are our guides for what to remember. If something is bland or predictable, it will be forgotten immediately, and will not change our brains. Many strong emotions result from dangerous events, like burning your hand in a fire. Emotion-influenced learning like this can happen very quickly—often from a single dramatic experience.

If something is repeated over and over, we gain a certain fluency through practice and rehearsal. Even dull repetition of routine tasks will strengthen the connections. If the experience is not repeated, its brain support will fade away and even disappear after a time. This process saves the energy required to maintain no-longer-useful abilities.

Building new neural circuits later in life is difficult because we have already built many fast and effective ones. These existing pathways, along with aging-related general decline, conspire to make it hard to acquire new abilities.

There is truth to the adage "You can't teach an old dog new tricks."

A quick reminder—the brain is not separate from the body. For long-term improvement in all mental functions, get voluntary exercise and adequate regular sleep. Exercise slows cognitive decline associated with aging, and has a strong antidepressant effect. It also acts as a buffer against physical and emotional stress. Exercise changes the very structure of the brain by multiplying the branching of smaller blood vessels. It also makes certain neuronal connections bushier.

Chapter 4
HOW WE LEARN AND REMEMBER

The purpose of memory

What is memory for?

If you think that the function of memory is to accurately remember all of your past life experiences, you are way off!

As you may remember (pun intended) from the last chapter, memory is not even necessary for life to exist. Nor is it required as part of the brain. Plenty of ancient creatures have done just fine without it.

Take a look at alligators—the basic design has worked unchanged for 200,000,000 years. The same is true of sharks—with recognizable ancestors stretching back 450,000,000 years. Both of these apex predators are largely a bundle of automatic reflexes and instincts. Their food sources have changed radically. But their ability to spot, kill, and eat other animals has worked reliably across vast periods.

The purpose of memory is to help you survive—not to be accurate.

Survival imperatives are the focus of memory, and will reliably influence us across all cultures and contexts. We will most easily remember how to avoid pain, find mating opportunities and the locations of food, and how to care for our young.

The bottom line is simple:

If something does not help us to improve our survival chances, it is useless and will not be remembered.

Stages of memory

There are several stages of memory and each has its unique considerations:

- **Encoding**—deciding which events to notice, and recognizing them as unified across separate sensory experiences
- **Storing**—saving events in short-term working memories, and more permanently by conscious repetition or consolidation during sleep
- **Retrieving**—accessing past experiences when related or similar situations occur
- **Forgetting**—maintaining only the most useful memories and fading the rest

Attention is a key concept which cuts across all of these stages. Distraction can easily undermine the encoding of information. Disturbed sleep can greatly affect the chances of successful storage. Tactics like closing your eyes to shut out competing visual inputs can improve the accuracy of retrieval.

Encoding

Want to create something memorable?

Combine emotion, novelty, and a multi-sensory experience to form stronger memories.

The vast majority of impressions we get from our environment don't have survival implications. It would take energy to think about them, or to act upon them. Our thrifty organism doesn't tolerate this kind of extravagant squandering of resources.

Our brain is a very powerful "ignoring machine" whose default is to do nothing.

Aversion or attraction alerts us to the events which matter. The stronger the associated emotions, the more memorable the event will be.

Sometimes even peak experiences become routine through repeated exposure. Adrenaline junkies who skydive never quite get the same "rush" on their 100th jump as they did on their first. Eventually such events are not required to be remembered, because they have "been there and done that" many times—the thrill is gone.

Imagine if a scary clown jumped out at you while you were walking up to your front door today. You would feel residual apprehension for a long time afterward, every time you approached your door.

Surprise and novelty make us pay attention and remember.

Do you remember ever riding on a rollercoaster? The rushing wind is whipping through your hair. Air is blasting through your nostrils. Your body is slammed by massive gravitational forces at unexpected angles. Your heart is beating violently. You are screaming and hearing the screams of your terrified fellow passengers all around you. Your vision is assaulted by wildly changing views and perspectives. And your inner ear is conspiring with your stomach to evacuate your lunch…

Now imagine watching someone on the same rollercoaster from a first-person point of view during a movie. Yes, it can still be quite visceral, and your mind will supply plenty of the associated sensations, as it simulates the experience. But it will not have nearly the same impact on you. It will be less likely to be remembered compared to your own richly encoded direct experience.

The more elaborately and vividly we encode a memory at the moment that we experience it, the stronger it will be.

Storage

It is important to distinguish between short-term "working" memory and long-term memories.

Working memory allows us to accomplish specific and immediate actions or tasks. It takes effort to maintain attention on such memories. For example, we can repeat something over and over, to maintain our focus. Short-term memory also has a very limited capacity. If we try to remember a list of items, we are limited to juggling approximately four.

Various techniques and practices can be used to enhance short-term memory. Some experts can extract higher-order groupings, and synthesize individual parts into larger "chunks." Others create multiple associations with each item, to connect to existing memories or concepts in the brain.

Repetition and rehearsal are the keys to storing memories and creating stronger associations.

When rehearsing lists of items, we will be more likely to remember the first items (primacy effect), and the last items (recency effect). We are least likely to retain the ones in the middle.

Primacy effects are usually stronger because the first item also serves as an "anchor" to which we compare later ones. For strictly memory-related tasks, the recency effect can be stronger since the very last thing we rehearsed is the freshest.

To convert our daily impressions into long-term memories, we need to sleep on them.

Sleep is critical to our well-being. Lack of it negatively impacts our attention, emotional state, reasoning, self-control, working memory, quantitative skills, and physical coordination.

From the perspective of memory, sleep consolidates and integrates new experiences with previous ones. What we experience in the hour before sleep is weighted several times more than the rest of the day's experiences combined. Think of it as a selective nightly update that overlays useful knowledge on our previous view of the world.

Retrieval

Retrieval of memories is intimately tied to how they were first encoded and stored. Since the encoding originally came through sensory channels, retrieving the memory can be tied to the circumstances in which you first experienced it. Time of day, place, and surrounding conditions are all brought to the retrieval process.

For example, listening to a song from your childhood can automatically bring the rich associations of where you first heard it. The sights, sounds, smells, and people of that long-ago time and place all spring back to life.

Smell is another strong memory trigger, and is the only sense which is directly connected to the brain. It bypasses the blood-brain barrier and intermediate structures of the central nervous system. This is tied to our ancestors' ability to avoid poisonous or spoiled food, and had very direct survival value.

Memory traces are partly stored in the same part of the brain where they were originally perceived. It is easiest to access them again under similar conditions.

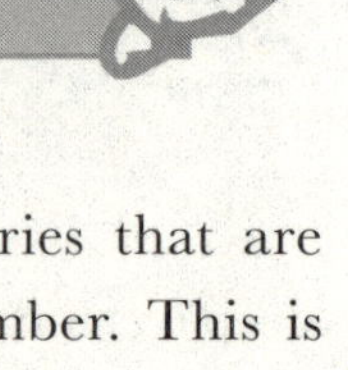

The quality of the storage will impact retrieval. Memories that are stored with significant repetition will be easiest to remember. This is especially true of ones that were also spaced out and encoded more elaborately.

Storing and recalling memories is easier when new sensory information is not competing for our attention.

Forgetting and distortion

What passes for memory is a fleeting dance of our consciousness. It is fickle, wildly inaccurate, and woefully incomplete.

We are flooded with overwhelming stimulation every second of our lives. Even if we could remember it all, it would require impossibly large amounts of storage and energy to maintain.

Yes, the brain senses and filters vast amounts of information. But it is an energy miser, and most of the time the right answer is for it to do nothing. Most information is not acted upon, nor stored for later retrieval. It is simply noise—a confirmation that nothing meaningful has changed in our environment. This ignoring process is ongoing every moment of our lives. It is completely unconscious. The brain is constantly hitting the "delete" button.

Forgetting is an essential survival strategy for the brain. It is a very effective "forgetting machine."

Forgetting allows us to preserve only what might enhance our survival prospects. Most memories disappear within minutes if they are not novel. Those that survive may strengthen after a good night's sleep, or when they are repeatedly accessed. But what we forget is not a conscious decision, and forgetting cannot be avoided.

Just because a memory is vivid, does not mean it's accurate.

The vast majority of memories will differ from the original experiences, and we will get the details wrong in most of them as well. That's even true when we are focused, and can be much more likely in the presence of outside distractions.

Both voluntary and involuntary social interactions can change our memories. A therapist can help us to reframe the meaning and importance of past events—thereby changing their vividness and our ability to remember them. An opposing lawyer during a cross-examination knows full well the power of subtle framing. Through this they often get the answers and responses they want from witnesses. Interrogators can wear down captives to fundamentally disconnect them from factual reality. Black is white and white is black—it is shocking how susceptible we are to the power of suggestion.

Sleep is needed to consolidate long-term memories, and combine them with similar previous ones. The most vivid and emotionally salient ones will be processed more strongly, as well as the most recent ones occurring shortly before sleep. But the regular overlays of our daily updates also wash away earlier impressions which are no longer useful. All memories fade over time. And the ones which remain are often shockingly inaccurate, or are incomplete caricatures of reality.

The "past" is a warped echo of itself. It plays out against forgetting, distortion, and the overlay of subsequent experiences. The "future" is only one possible mental simulation of what might happen. We rerun it against changing circumstances to optimize our chances of survival. Both are fantasies. The mind tells itself comforting lies because it wants to survive. We need to hang on to our cherished illusions in order not to slip into despair.

There is no detailed life recording

I am sorry to disappoint science fiction fans who are waiting to download our essence into some sort of permanent digital equivalent. There is no ability to rewind our life in reverse, with every movie frame exact and uncorrupted.

Most of our experiences are handled by the primal parts of the brain on autopilot. Those instinctual and automatic responses do not require memory and are ignored.

The ones which are handled by the memory system are not truly memories at all. Rather, they are a combination of our current senses, twisted recollections of vivid past experiences that fade over time, and mental simulations of the future created by our dreams and waking thoughts. Together this creates our current state.

There is no area of the brain where an accurate recording of our life events exists.

Chapter 5

THIS IS YOUR BRAIN ON DRUGS

Emotions are signposts for survival

People often consider their conscious, rational, and verbal thoughts to be the whole of their reality. The reason we undervalue emotions is that they often appear random, act on us instantly, and can't be immediately described before we react.

Emotions originate in the *limbic system* portion of the brain where verbal speech does not operate. Language processing happens in the cortex—the evolutionarily newer part of the brain. However, the cortex does not release *any* of the neurochemicals which cause emotions and underlie all your decisions.

The cortex can occasionally override the limbic system. But this is only a momentary effect and quickly depletes our very small reserves of conscious attention and self-control.

Repetition and emotion—the two key ways to learn

Learning, memory, behavior, and habits are all tied together. We can build new behaviors through repetition or emotionally significant events. The repetition method reinforces the relationship between a behavior and a particular outcome—gradually and uneventfully building stronger associations.

Strong emotions cause a chemical reaction that can rewire the brain instantly.

Even a single emotionally charged event can trigger a long-lasting, immediate rewiring of the brain. A strong emotional experience will instantly lock in the event, and encode the related circumstances as either good or bad. This new information will be used as we react to similar situations in the future. Once these strong associations are established, it is difficult to undo them later in life. We have learned through our environment to consider certain events as painful, and others as pleasurable.

Strong emotions are only linked to things which we learned to associate with survival.

The brain requires massive energy to operate properly, and can direct the body to expend even more energy. Unless we are pulled by pleasure or pushed by pain, the very strong default behavior is to do nothing—to conserve energy.

If it feels good, go towards it. If feels bad, avoid it. If it's benign, do nothing.

"It feels good" is encoded by chemicals like dopamine, various endorphins, oxytocin, and serotonin. "It feels bad" is triggered by stress hormones like cortisol. The lifespan of the happy chemicals circulating inside of you is very short—a few seconds or minutes at a time. Your brain spurts these happy chemicals to focus you on something that increases your chances of survival. Afterward it shuts off the flow—conserving energy and resetting for the next motivational opportunity.

Happy chemicals quickly get shut off by the brain—so they can be triggered again when needed in the future.

So far, we have been talking about the quality of emotions—either positive ones which we want to repeat, or negative ones which we want to avoid. However, there is another way of looking at emotions—their strength.

The intensity of emotions tells us when something is salient, and that we should pay attention.

A dampening of emotions, or ennui (a lack of interest in experiences or sensations) is the opposite of salience. It can be seen in mental health conditions such as depression, when the response to all events attenuates.

The treadmill of unhappiness

There is no such thing as permanent happiness. Our brains are designed to continuously scan for dangers. Being on alert causes stress and unhappiness. We are nudged by happy chemicals when appropriate, but if we want more of them, we have to keep doing something to trigger them again. This leads to an endless cycle of escalation. The quest for happy chemicals will lead eventually to the release of the unhappy ones.

There is even more bad news. The brain cares about the survival of our genes—not necessarily of our bodies. For example, if you hurt yourself in the process of mating, the tradeoff may very well be worth it to your brain. Even if you died in the attempt, your genes had an opportunity to propagate.

Bad feelings are produced by cortisol.

When we feel bad, we will immediately start scanning for ways to make the bad feelings stop. Sometimes there are no obvious resolutions or clear ways forward.

What makes us feel good is based partly on our specific past experiences.

Most people like ice cream. But if you had never tried ice cream before, you would simply not have a positive association with it. So eating ice cream would not be a response you would choose if you were feeling bad and wanted to comfort yourself.

As I mentioned, it is possible for your cortex to occasionally intervene and override your impulses. But in general, you will look for the quickest way to get a hit of the happy chemicals, and make your bad feelings go away. Those pathways in the brain are very strong and their operation often feels effortless. In most cases you will succeed at triggering the happy chemicals.

That's when the real trouble begins.

Once the quick effect of happy chemicals wears off, we want more, and have to do more to get them. This cycle leads, in time, to side effects. As we repeat this process, we get more side effects. These eventually build until they start to trigger unhappy chemicals.

It is a cruel joke.

The more cortisol you produce as a result of the side effects, the more you go back to the same behavior. It becomes a vicious feedback loop that becomes easier and easier to trigger. You may release happy and unhappy chemicals at the same time—wrestling with each other for control of your behavior. But there is no way to make the unhappy chemicals stop—the brain's imperative is survival, not some lifetime of bliss for you.

You are stuck on this merry-go-round.

Altered states

Many animals get drunk and stoned.

Although it is hard to study this in the wild, there are dozens of species that like to get buzzed. They take full advantage of a variety of natural intoxicants and psychoactive compounds occurring in plants and fungi. Deer act goofy after gorging on fermented apples at orchards. There are unmated male fruit flies that prefer alcohol more strongly than their sexually satisfied counterparts. The Bohemian waxwing birds of Canada get so plastered on the fermented berries of the rowan tree that they can no longer fly.

Our shared brain development makes us susceptible to the influence of the same compounds whenever they are available. Since we share addictive brain circuits with very ancient insect cousins, perhaps it's time to stop talking about "lifestyle choices" among humans.

We will focus on the happy chemicals (dopamine, endorphins, oxytocin, and serotonin) in the next chapter. But let's pause to consider the basic range of natural and artificial chemicals available to people.

The ones impacting the brain are called psychoactive compounds. These include stimulants, sedatives, opiates, hallucinogens, and drugs which have a mixture of effects. Many of them activate the *medial forebrain pleasure circuit* and intimately involve dopamine. However, there are several classes of drugs that work on different parts of the brain, and have other psychoactive compounds at their core.

The brain naturally creates some endorphins as its own form of morphine. Morphine and its cousins heroin, opium, and fentanyl produce euphoria. But they do not work through dopamine signaling directly. The effects of this system influence pain perception, mood, memory, appetite, and control of the digestive system.

Cannabis's key active ingredient is THC and has unique receptors in the brain. Natural endocannabinoids produced in the body modulate communication between neurons. They dampen the strength of the response. Throwing this system off balance by overloading it with potent external THC has far-reaching effects like memory loss, impaired coordination, and slowed reaction time. Thinking, judgment, pain sensitivity, and sensation are also altered. Resulting feelings of euphoria or panic are possible.

Tobacco's key psychoactive ingredient is nicotine. It binds to specific sites that evolved to handle the naturally occurring neurotransmitter acetylcholine. Although its psychoactive function is not well understood, memory, arousal, and attention are all affected by it.

Alcohol's psychoactive effects are even more complicated. It increases the secretion of both endorphins and endocannabinoids. The effect is to inhibit certain dopamine neurons.

The arc of addiction

As you have seen above, pleasure is central to some but not all psychoactive drugs. There is also a wide range of addiction potential. Drugs which strongly activate dopamine in the medial forebrain pleasure circuit are the ones with the highest risk of addiction. These include heroin, amphetamines like meth, and cocaine.

Drugs that weakly activate this pleasure circuit carry smaller risks of addiction. Cannabis and alcohol fall into this category.

Drugs that don't activate the pleasure circuit at all carry less risk of addiction. These include mescaline, LSD, SSRI antidepressants, and benzodiazepines.

But there is more to the addiction picture.

The mode and frequency of drug delivery matter a lot.

How potent is the drug? How quickly does it build up? How frequently is the use repeated?

After all, you can, and some people do, chew tobacco. But the instant delivery of vaporized nicotine to the bloodstream via the lungs is a much more effective method. Each puff is also a frequent "learning event"—building associations and strengthening neural connections.

You can also eat opium. But injected heroin is much more addictive. It can cross cell membranes more easily than morphine, and produces a more intense pleasure rush. At the same time, injection delivers it immediately into the bloodstream—resulting in a higher "high."

> Addiction is the ongoing and compulsive use of a drug in the face of increasingly negative consequences.

Addicts can destroy their health, ruin relationships, and sabotage their careers and finances. They will even risk death—all in the name of their drugs of choice.

This process unfolds in well-defined stages.

The initial exposure produces delightful and seemingly positive effects. Depending on the drug, some combination of well-being, calmness, alertness, expansiveness, clarity, energy, or euphoria results.

Of course, that makes the user want it more. However, when they come back for another taste, drug tolerance quickly develops. They will need a higher and higher dose to feel the same effect. As they become a regular user, this tolerance grows.

At some point it is impossible, despite dose increases, to even maintain the original level of high or pleasure. Once the trajectory of addiction takes hold, pleasure is suppressed, and wanting or need takes its place.

Users begin to feel bad in its absence. A sense of physical dependence can manifest as irritability, depression, and the inability to concentrate. Going too long without the drug can also bring on physical effects like chills, nausea, cramps, and sweating. They feel strong cravings. These are often triggered by environmental cues such as surroundings, time of day, and companions.

> Pleasure circuits are there to help you survive, and to repeat experiences that lead you towards important goals.

Weak versions of many addictive compounds are naturally produced in the body. They help you to carry out experiences which enhance survival prospects.

Unfortunately, when we turn to external sources of drugs, we are overpowering the system. We are co-opting the pleasure circuits with super-potent synthetics and novel delivery systems. This leads to a deep need to repeat the experiences. The cravings are bound up with drug-associated mental states and external circumstances. They are strongly activated whenever getting the drugs becomes a possibility again. Many addicts relapse even by taking a small dose after abstinence. They will get a pleasure rush even stronger than their initial use due to an effect called drug sensitization.

The bottom line is devastating.

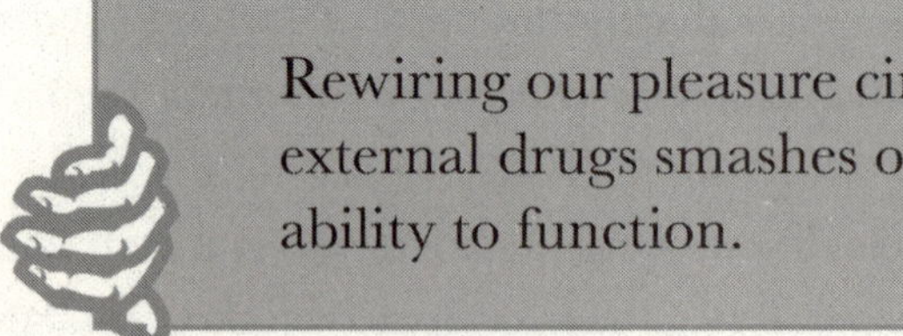

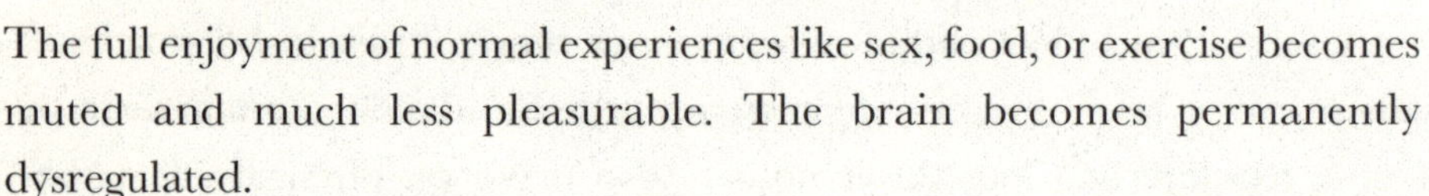

The full enjoyment of normal experiences like sex, food, or exercise becomes muted and much less pleasurable. The brain becomes permanently dysregulated.

Feeding and energy balance

Let's rewind hundreds of millions of years. One of the basic attributes that all life shares is the need for energy. Basic mechanisms for balancing the energy system have been extremely varied. Sometimes animals sleep. Sometimes they fight to the death for mating opportunities. Sometimes they hibernate and go dormant to survive the harsh environment.

The control point for feeding (and sex, aggression, body temperature, and drinking) is a portion of the brain called the *hypothalamus*. Think of it as the master overseer of how we choose to gather, store, and use our energy in the pursuit of changing survival goals.

Our evolution as a species was based on small hunter-gatherer formations. We were constantly on the move. To be effective at this, we had to balance two competing needs. If you got too skinny, you would drop dead during the next extended period of food scarcity. If you got too fat, you would not be very mobile, and would be unable to carry out critical daily tasks. You could not hunt for food as effectively, or keep up with your fast-moving cousins on the march.

Each person has a body-fat set point. We can't deviate from this set point for very long.

I know this is bad news for the dieters out there. Body fat percentages are just one of the many such homeostasis systems in the body. A rebalancing equilibrium occurs to keep key functions within a specific normal range. Examples include temperature, blood pressure, hydration, pH levels, blood glucose, and breathing.

Whatever your set point is, you are stuck with it. Eighty percent of the variation in body weight is controlled by your genes. This is about the same hereditary percentage as for height. Yet you rarely hear someone suggest that you "drop a little height"

When fat weight is gained, a hormone called leptin is released into the bloodstream. This happens in proportion to the amount of total fat in your body. In the brain, the high levels of leptin will signal the hypothalamus to lower your appetite and to increase energy expenditure. When you lose fat, the system works in reverse—increasing appetite and reducing energy use based on the lowered leptin levels in the blood. This equilibrium setpoint makes it hard to lose fat and keep it off. The farther you are away from the setpoint, the stronger the drives will feel to return to equilibrium.

Of course, there are also short-term eating signals. Our bodies are smart enough to detect the amount of energy available in the food—not just its volume. Stomach lining cells can signal the brain about the chemical and mechanical properties of the food that we eat. How distended our gut feels is another indication of being satiated. But leptin levels are the guardians of long-term body fat, and do their job very well.

Food and emotions

Our evolutionary diet was mostly vegetarian, with very little fats or sugars. If foods were more moist or oily, we could swallow them more easily. People would eat more food if they didn't have to work too hard to chew or swallow it. We rarely tasted anything sweet.

High-density energy sources were rare—whether it was an occasional ripe fruit, or a chunk of dead animal. We did not know when we might find such a treasure next. If we ran across them, we would gorge—storing up energy for the inevitable lean times. We are programmed at birth to prefer certain tastes and smells. Many of these are associated with sugars, fats, and salt.

We get pleasure from high fat and high sugar combo foods, and will gorge on them.

Eating produces a wave of dopamine. When you combine fat and sugar, you get a super-addictive dopamine combination. Our bodies did not evolve to properly handle this once-scarce energy resource.

Weight gain can be exacerbated by stress. Stress-based overeating of "comfort foods" results in fat gain, especially around the stomach. The goal is to prepare for future increased energy requirements during unpredictable times.

However, the opposite seems to happen under conditions of super-high stress. We stop wanting to eat. This mode seems to be closer to the "freeze" response. Immediate survival is the dominant concern, and the long-term energy reserve is a distant second as a consideration.

Drugs that block dopamine receptors also increase appetite and fat gain. The opposite is true when drugs similar to dopamine are administered. Such *dopamine receptor agonists* suppress appetite. Natural interventions for stress reduction can also have a similar effect. Activities such as exercise and meditation reduce stress hormone surges and overeating.

Chapter 6
THE CHEMISTRY OF HAPPINESS

Older and newer brain chemicals

Four important brain compounds feature prominently in evolutionary psychology. They can be thought of as pleasurable or "happy" chemicals. Two of them are more ancient, and support basic survival skills. We share dopamine with fruit flies and very primitive forms of life going back hundreds of millions of years. Dopamine helps to motivate us and expend energy in the pursuit of rewards. Endorphins help to temporarily block out pain, so we can survive battles and immediate existential crises.

Motivation and managing pain are universal life needs. Smaller animal brains function largely with these kinds of basic responses. Animals with bigger brains also incorporate their specific life experiences into their actions.

Since mammals need the safety of the herd to survive, two other happy chemicals also emerged. Oxytocin helps us to bond with our young, shepherd them through helpless childhoods, and fight against outsider threats. Serotonin helps us to navigate the ever-shifting dominance hierarchies within our tribal group.

As we discussed in the last chapter, cortisol is the stress chemical that we try to neutralize by releasing the happy chemicals. Adrenaline is also triggered in stressful situations—preparing us to either fight, flee, or freeze as appropriate. It is an amplifier which prepares us for immediate action.

Dopamine—motivation and energy control

Many people have reduced dopamine's function to simply being a "feel good" chemical. This inaccurate and crude definition misses its crucial evolutionary purposes.

As we have already seen, the main function of the brain is to navigate a changing world. To do this effectively, animals and insects need to be able to accomplish two things. They must decide when to invest versus when to conserve energy. They must also keep their mental model of the world updated and as accurate as possible.

Dopamine allows us to decide when to use energy and when to conserve it.

The brain is a very energy-intensive system. It can also trigger voluntary movements of the body. These may require additional massive energy expenditures like running and fighting. You can saunter to pick up and examine a plant. But chasing a small animal will require significant energy output. Energy control is critical to the brain's success.

Dopamine supplies motivation, and signals us to use energy when there is an expectation of a valuable reward.

The effects of dopamine and the positive emotions it triggers are based on your past experience. Your brain only focuses on what is scarce and important to your survival. This depends on your current environment and past life experience.

If you are in the desert without water, even a remote hint of plant life will motivate you to explore in a certain direction. But if you live on the banks of a river, dopamine will not be released in a quest for water, since it is readily available. If something is common and falls into our lap without much effort, it can be taken for granted and largely ignored.

Dopamine will not be triggered by common or easily available rewards.

Dopamine is metered out in a miserly fashion. If everything is on track towards achieving a particular goal, little nudges of it are enough to keep us moving forward. If there is no urgency or need to record new ways of getting rewards, the dopamine flow stops. Dopamine is about anticipation.

Updating our mental model

Okay, you got your reward—now what?

Dopamine motivated you to reach it. But it also helped you to remember and store all the associated information in your updated mental model. In the future, you will be able to more easily spot the conditions under which a similar reward might be available.

After each achieved goal we automatically do the following:

- Get a surge of pleasure—immediate liking of the experience
- Remember sensory and environmental cues—sights, locations, sounds, and smells preceding and overlapping with the experience
- Note internal states—our feelings and thoughts at the time
- Decide how much we liked the reward—allowing us to prioritize among competing goals, and metering how much effort and risk to expend in their future pursuit

Dopamine helps update our mental model of the world—to make reaching the same goal easier in the future.

Dopamine-releasing neurons are constantly making predictions about how the world will function. They generate pleasure every time their predictions are correct. These predictions are based on the current mental model.

But our models of the world are often wrong. Every time we come upon something unfamiliar or make a mistake, our brain adjusts. The neurons measure the difference between our expectations and the actual results. Our errors serve as a guide. Mistakes are not something to be avoided. Each post-mistake adjustment improves our performance in the future.

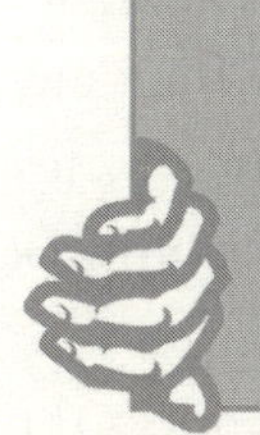

By using prediction mistakes and errors to improve performance, the brain turns repeated failure into a better model of the world.

We need to continually train our dopamine-releasing neurons. If we don't, their ability to accurately predict declines. Making sure that our gut instincts are right requires constant and deliberate practice. Someone who is an "expert" at something is often the person who has put in the most time seeing subtle and repeated variations of an experience. Eventually, their intuition becomes an accurate feeling which can be conjured on demand.

Surprise creates an emergency in the brain. Something which surprises us is, by definition, something that we did not effectively predict. This can pose a threat to our survival. Imagine a bear charged at you five times faster than you were expecting—not the kind of surprise many of your ancestors would have survived…

Surprises trigger the "Oh crap!" circuit in the brain and cause immediate and far-reaching responses.

As soon as a prediction error is recognized, your brain kicks into action. It immediately stops the flow of dopamine and rings the alarm bell. The *anterior cingulate cortex* (ACC) is a brain area rich in dopamine neurons. It's responsible for acting on dopamine prediction errors. The ACC instantly sends out a unique electrical signal called the "error-related negativity."

The ACC is also rich in spindle neuron cells. Unlike their short bushy cousins, these cells are long and slender and connect to the rest of the cortex. They only exist in great apes, although humans have 40 times more spindle cells than any other primate. This suggests a connection to higher thinking. The spindle neuron transmits electrical signals faster than any other type. Their high density in people instantly alerts the whole cortex and makes it pay undivided attention to the surprise. It's all-hands-on-deck when dealing with the unexpected!

Some people have a genetic mutation in the ACC which reduces the number of dopamine receptors. In effect, these people have a much harder time learning from their mistakes. They are also much more likely to get addicted to drugs and alcohol.

The pleasure circuit in more detail

Dopamine pleasure-based motivation is very strong in rats. Genetically speaking, they are our very close mammalian cousins. Rats would prefer self-administered dopamine "hits" to eating food when hungry or drinking water when thirsty. They ignore mating opportunities with in-heat females and endure physical electroshock pain. They even stop caring for their young. Powerful stuff indeed!

The pleasure circuit encompasses the ventral tegmental area (VTA), the medial forebrain bundle, the septum, the nucleus accumbens, and parts of the thalamus and hypothalamus. From the VTA, dopamine-releasing connections exist to several brain areas. These govern emotions, memory of facts and events, habits, learning, judgment, and planning.

Dopamine is quickly vacuumed up and stored again for later reuse. This happens through the action of *dopamine transporter* compounds. Drugs like amphetamines and cocaine interfere with the natural action of dopamine transporters. The result is a longer-lasting and more intense pleasure signal. Some psychoactive drugs artificially activate dopamine receptors. As we have previously discussed, this can lead to self-destructive addictions.

Sometimes dopamine cells are destroyed. Dopamine receptors can also be blocked by drugs known as *dopamine receptor antagonists*. Under such circumstances, the desire to chase rewards and pleasures decreases or completely dies away. This is the case in Parkinson's disease—which is known to result in the loss of dopamine-containing cells in two key brain areas. The only known treatments involve increasing the circulating dopamine levels. This compensates for the smaller number of dopamine-containing neurons.

Low levels of dopamine result in a lowered activation of the pleasure circuit. This also lowers novelty-seeking behaviors and reduces the risk of addiction. If the low levels of dopamine are corrected in Parkinson's patients, they often find themselves at higher risk for uncontrolled gambling, risky behaviors, addiction, and a variety of other impulse-control disorders. As soon as the dose of treatment is lowered, these behavioral changes also fade away.

The dopamine-based pleasure circuit is involved in a wide variety of activities such as eating sweet and fatty foods, obtaining money, using psychoactive drugs, and sexual orgasm. Exercise, mindfulness practices such as meditation, prayer, social approval, and giving to charity also trigger it.

Compulsive gambling runs in families—although it is more common in men than women. Gambling is often tied to other pleasure-related and impulse-control behaviors. Indeed, there is a ten times higher incidence of alcoholism among gamblers, and a six times higher rate of nicotine addiction. Winning less strongly activates the dopamine-rich areas of the brain for gambling addicts. The common thread through all of this is dopamine, and a blunted response to pleasure.

There may be evolutionary reasons for this decreased dopamine response in some individuals. Animals that are faced with indecision may take on extra risks to find more reliable predictors of important events.

Endorphins—emergency pain suppression

You did not hear the tiger sneak up on you...

The giant paw, edged with dagger-sized claws, knocked you down like a massive club and left deep bloody gashes across your back.

What should you do next?

- Focus on the pain and tend to your wounds, or
- Get up and run for your life—not feeling the pain at all

Your ancestors were able to do the latter—thanks to endorphins.

Many of us have heard about endorphins in the context of "runner's high." This is a floating mildly euphoric feeling long-distance runners sometimes experience after pushing through the initial pain. But endorphins did not evolve to motivate you to inflict intentional pain on your body. Their very purpose is to get away from more-immediate pain!

Endorphins mask physical pain for a short time—giving an injured animal a chance to reach safety.

The oblivion and ability to ignore your grave wounds is a welcome gift in deadly circumstances. Yes, you might die from untended wounds eventually. But you will definitely die if you do not deal with the immediate situation.

Endorphins are designed to quickly wear off. They are a counterpoint to pain for narrow specific circumstances. However, pain itself has a massive survival value. We evolved to notice and respond to pain signals—not to mask them regularly.

Strong social experiences, such as laughing or crying, also trigger endorphins mildly.

Oxytocin—attachment and outgroups

Oxytocin and similar compounds have been traced to lifeforms 400 million years ago. Yet, I think of it as the most archetypical of mammalian brain chemicals. Mammals are different from earlier animals due to a combination of our investment in our young and the instinct to cooperate in groups or herds.

An alligator does not need a group around it and is efficient in getting its needs met. If it encounters another animal, chances are it is an enemy, or food, or both. Birds care for their young. But their dedication to hatching an egg and some quick feedings can't be compared to the demands on mammals. The devotion of mammal parents extends to intensively caring for their offspring over the years or even decades.

Attachment is at the core of mammalian experience.

We mammals care for our children. This makes it possible for them to be born completely helpless and without the means to survive on their own for extended periods. Yet, this is a very risky reproductive strategy. We have relatively few children, and have a massive investment in each one—feeling profound grief if we lose them.

Unlike the millions of spawn a fish may produce, mammal parents attach to their particular children much more profoundly. Before the baby is born, oxytocin is released, and the mother is bonded to the newborn. The hormone aids in contractions and the birth process itself, as well as lactation and nursing. In a very real sense, the mammal female does not become a mother until the moment of this oxytocin flood. Through it she is transformed instantly into a nurturing selfless servant—catering to the endless needs of the newborn.

The baby, in turn, is bonded strongly to the mother with the same hormone. And it needs to be—since it is completely helpless by itself. If this secure attachment does not happen it would not command the necessary attention to develop and thrive. Parents interacting with their babies causes the infants' oxytocin levels to rise, creating a virtuous feedback loop of care.

Oxytocin immediately bonds a mammal mother and child at birth, and promotes a nurturing relationship.

Eventually, this oxytocin-based attachment transfers from the mother to the larger pack. Mammals operate in groups because there is safety in numbers. They may be individually weaker, but can cooperate to survive.

Mammals release the stress hormone cortisol when we are not within sight of any members of our group. We are weak when isolated, and the larger group provides protection. We seek to return to the safety of the herd and are rewarded with oxytocin when we do.

If you trust another member of the group or enjoy their trust in you, you are ensuring group survival. The social alliances built among group members are critical. The building of such bonds is rewarded with good feelings by oxytocin.

Several activities promote oxytocin production, and foster trust as a result. These include touch and grooming, experiencing emotional support, and orgasm.

Bonding and caretaking behaviors cement social alliances within the mammal group.

Oxytocin is popularly known as the "love drug" or "cuddle hormone" for the reasons described above. But it has a sharp edge that separates the ingroup members from those who are enemies or outsiders. The loving mother bear who tends her cubs will become a raging and aggressive monster if outsiders get near. And the flip side of tribal group cohesion is aggression towards competing groups—driven by a heightened hatred of them.

Oxytocin brings familiars closer, but fosters aggression against outsider enemies.

Most mammals operate on this simple model—you are either in the ingroup, or in the outgroup. People have a third mode. Someone may be an ally or an enemy, or they may be a stranger with unknown intentions towards us.

Normally we carefully watch strangers for the smallest hint of their plans and desired relationship to us.

The drug MDMA, also known as "molly" or "ecstasy" in its street form, is popular for its feel-good properties at raves. It produces a number of prosocial effects—putting us in a positive and trusting mood around strangers. It reduces anxiety and increases empathy, while lowering recognition of anger and sadness in others. As you may have guessed, the mechanism behind this is MDMA's ability to increase oxytocin. In effect, it temporarily moves neutral strangers into the ingroup category.

Serotonin—social dominance and hierarchy

Anyone with a sibling knows that there is always conflict and jockeying for position and advantage even within families. Oxytocin promotes ingroup cooperation against outsiders. But it does not solve the problems of hierarchy formation and competition within the group.

There is a saying about sled dog teams. "If you are not the lead dog, the view is always the same."

There are many advantages to being at the top of the social hierarchy. Dominance provides more security, more food, and better mating opportunities. Every species has a preliminary qualifying event before mating. For mammals, this is often the achievement of dominance goals. Mammals with higher status and numerous allies have more surviving offspring.

Being on the outskirts of the group is hard. You will probably have fewer mating opportunities and limited access to food. You will be in the most vulnerable position when it comes to outsider threats.

But there is no free lunch if you want the top spot. You have to fight your way to it, or spend time building durable alliances. Tremendous energy is expended in the pursuit of dominance and respect or in threats to your social standing. If you have any extra resources as a mammal, it is wise to invest them in developing social power which might help you survive tomorrow.

> Serotonin results in the feeling of wellness and security knowing that your needs will be met in the group.

When a mammal achieves high social status, their serotonin levels rise, while those of subordinates decrease. But life at the top is never fun. If a lower-ranking mammal feels desperate enough, a cortisol spike will drive them to improve their current situation. Staying at the top is a constant struggle.

Happiness gone wrong

The positive feelings from happy brain chemicals can be hijacked or distorted. Under certain circumstances, they no longer serve their intended purpose. They can actually work against our long-term well-being.

Finding threats can make you feel good. Imagine you are in a forest on a camping trip. You know that a dangerous wolf is stalking your party, because you can hear its terrifying howling in the darkness nearby. Once you spot the wolf, you feel safer. The evidence of a wolf that you sought is rewarded by dopamine after the sighting. You also get an oxytocin boost from protecting your fellow campers against an outside threat, and a serotonin bump from the feeling of being right. For some people, being a negative prophet of doom has its upside and can be a self-reinforcing pattern.

Remember, happy chemicals are not there to create a life of permanent bliss. They are only supposed to be available in short bursts to direct us towards survival goals and behaviors.

If you try to trigger ongoing happy feelings, you will run into increasingly disappointing negative side effects.

We often respond to disappointment by repeating the behavior. We trigger the side effects again—often in a stronger form. We get what we want, or we get the lesson with redoubled force, and the cumulative effects of consequences. Unfortunately, sometimes we need to get a shovel-smash to the face before we are ready to learn.

We have already covered the cruel arc of drug addiction and its permanent rewiring of the brain. When powerful compounds not synthesized within our own body are available, they trick us into going down a dead-end path. Opiates can trigger the euphoria of natural endorphins, without the trauma of the preceding physical damage. But they lead to such a degree of lethargy that some addicts neglect personal care to a shocking degree. Natural endorphins evolved for extremely rare and short-lasting responses to life-and-death emergencies. Strong synthetic versions are used as an artificial path to bliss.

Happiness chemicals can lead us down a counterproductive path even without external drugs.

Being "in love" is one of the most powerful happiness payoffs. It combines the following chemicals into a drug cocktail:

- Dopamine—the rewards of "the chase" and finally getting the object of your courtship, as well as from the buildup to sexual orgasms
- Oxytocin—physical touch and the resulting well-being from protecting the new member of your ingroup
- Serotonin—improved social standing resulting from your new alliance with your partner

But romantic infatuation does not last. Remember, dopamine will not keep firing in the presence of a familiar or easily accessible reward. Despite your delusion about this love lasting forever, any relationship eventually becomes the "new normal." Once the dopamine delivery stops, many people go looking for the same high in the newness and excitement of chasing another person.

Dopamine is only triggered by new rewards.

You need to keep chasing newness of experience, possession, or environment to keep it flowing. One common maladaptation is the need to hoard things—always seeking the next object for your collection. Another is to travel—regularly rewarding your senses with exciting and unfamiliar adventures. These activities have predictable endgames—compulsive hoarding, or becoming an experience junky.

Oxytocin kept your ancestors from wandering away from the safety of the tribe every time somebody pissed them off. The prospects of any mammal trying to survive by itself are greatly diminished. However, not all groups are worth belonging to. Our need to stay in the group can lead to negative consequences.

Gangs are an unfortunate byproduct of this oxytocin dynamic. People join them seeking safety and protection. They bond over shared activities and rally in aggression against rival gangs. As a result, they form powerful attachments. However, the dynamic within the group can also be ruthless. Conflict is a routine part of all primate life. Gang members can turn on each other and fight for dominance. Members end up tolerating brutal behaviors and pain from the group rather than risk losing their friends. No matter how dysfunctional their behaviors may be, they can feel good about themselves because they are surrounded by allies.

Status within your group keeps serotonin flowing. Looking for recognition is a normal part of human life, even though it can lead to disappointment. No matter how much recognition you may have gotten in the past, you will feel bad if it stops. When others get the recognition which you crave, you look for ways to feel better. This search makes you repeat any actions which may have gotten you recognition in the past. Some behaviors like bullying, shaming, or undermining others can lead to very negative fallout.

Certain serotonin seekers turn to the role of being a hero and saving others. To fulfill their own need to rescue, they often reward and enable the negative behavior which requires rescuing in the first place.

Winning the love of a higher-status person is a common way to get a serotonin bump. We recognize the negative connotations of such activities. You are probably familiar with the sycophantic "butt kisser," the "gold digger" trying to land a rich mate, or a "groupie" who follows athletes, musicians, and politicians around. They are hoping to catch the eye of the high-status object of their desire. Even the smallest hint of resulting attention will spike serotonin.

PART II

REPTILES AND SHREWS

Chapter 7

THE AUTOPILOT AND THE POWER OF PAIN

Let's recap life on the planet: bacteria, viruses, cells, plants, insects, and animals. The latter two are the only ones which move. As we discovered earlier, the brain is necessary for dealing with fast-changing movement through the world. Some of the basic brain chemicals, like dopamine, are shared between us and lifeforms going back several hundred million years.

Moving lifeforms took two basic evolutionary paths: independence and interdependence.

The *independent* branch generally shares the following characteristics:

- Mature and functional at birth or shortly after
- Many more offspring over their lifetime
- Little or no investment in a particular child
- Operate independently for large parts of their life (except for mating events)

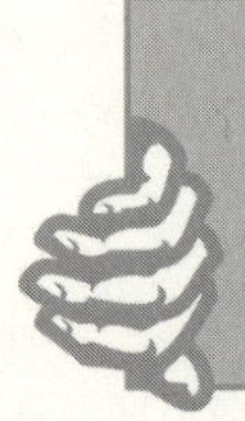

A wide variety of egg-laying reptiles, birds, and insects embody the more ancient independent approach.

The *interdependent* branch can be spotted by the following:

- Immature offspring incapable of survival for long periods after birth
- Fewer and less frequent offspring
- Significant or massive investment in each particular child
- Dependence on the extended group for survival and protection

Mammals epitomize the evolutionarily newer interdependent approach.

Mammals significantly overlapped in time with earlier independent species. We continue to live side by side with them. Earlier independent lifeforms still abound, including reptiles, birds, and lizards. The big die-off of dinosaurs allowed an explosion of mammalian varieties about 65 million years ago. But our early shrew cousins have existed for over 200 million years. They had diversified into several sub-branches by 100 million years ago.

I am sure paleobiologists will quibble with my definition and find exceptions. Emperor penguins in Antarctica tirelessly trek across the ice and steadfastly stand vigil over their eggs to keep them warm. They also congregate in large groups for extended periods. But for our purposes the distinction is informative, so I will continue to talk about mammals and reptiles as representative of the two.

The reptile brain—avoiding harm and ignoring most events

You don't need to learn to avoid harm.

Much of harm avoidance and survival can be accomplished by a few automatic responses.

Here are some examples:

- If it moves and is smaller than me, it might be food and I should chase it
- If it moves and is larger than me, it is a threat and I should run away from it
- If I feel pain and another animal is nearby, it is the cause of the pain and I should fight with it or move away
- If there are no threats around me, I should rest and do nothing

Modern human brains learn and adapt to our individual life experiences. But there is no need for the lizard brain to modify its responses. The next time a small creature is nearby, it is still likely to be a food source. The same automatic pre-programmed response still works and does not need to change.

The reptile brain is an ignoring machine.

The superpower of the reptile brain is efficiency and low energy requirements. At the heart of this is its ability to ignore events and minimize purposeful effort.

Here is the basic operating system of this primitive brain:

- Not dangerous? Ignore
- Not exciting and new? Ignore
- New? Summarize the gist, and ignore details
- Unexpected? Ignore and kick it upstairs to the newer brain parts to handle

There is a wondrous simplicity in this setup. Unless something is an emergency, the reptile brain conserves precious resources. This includes the energy needed to run the brain, as well as instructions to the body to initiate physical movement and expend even more energy. The crocodile will lie submerged unmoving in a river for hours, and in one violent lunge kill a passing animal which may take a week to digest. This is the ultimate in do-nothing efficiency!

Survival imperatives focus us on the real emergencies. They call for black-and-white decisions involving simple choices. They deal with the concrete and tangible, and the immediate here-and-now. None of this necessarily involves learning.

Fear and unhappiness

We previously looked at the "happy" chemicals, and only mentioned the "unhappy" stress chemical of cortisol in passing. Happy chemicals do not play a big role in the world of the reptile—it is almost exclusively driven by fear.

Cortisol is the emergency alert system of the brain—something is wrong and you need to do something about it!

The feeling-good chemicals were layered on later and enabled a wider variety of complex behaviors. But the fear and stress responses are enough to keep many animals alive. Pain avoidance is the strongest motivator for action, and a powerful memory aid for what to avoid in the future.

It is wrong to think of cortisol as the cause of unnecessary pain, when in fact its job is to prevent even greater pain.

The events and circumstances that occur just before the pain are etched into the brain. This "buffer memory" does not hold a lot of information. But it provides an instant of automatic advance recognition—allowing you to avoid similar threats in the future.

The brain borrows and reuses old evolutionary structures. There is a lot of overlap between the areas which store physical, emotional, and financial pain.

When you are on high alert, you will experience temporary effects that will help you in the short term. These include increased heart rate, lung capacity, and more blood flow to your limbs to boost voluntary movements. But this system was designed to function in short bursts—not continuously. Under ongoing chronic stress, bad things will start to happen. You may experience insomnia, depression, weakened immunity, and a higher risk of heart disease. If its flow is not stopped, cortisol will also damage parts of the brain needed for memory.

Sore losers

Our primal brain focuses on the choices which minimize pain and loss. As we will explore later, fear of losing will motivate us more than an opportunity to win. This originates in the amygdala, a part of the brain which encodes events that produce emotional reactions. The stronger the emotion, the easier and more permanently the related events will be remembered and stored in our long-term memory.

We notice and pay extra attention to anything which might result in pain or loss to us.

Chapter 8
DEMYSTIFYING RISK

Choices and actions are all about risk and reward.

In traditional economics "utility theory" the assumption is people will always act as "rational agents". Supposedly, they take the course of action which would maximize the payoff available to them under the circumstances. The evolutionary reality of taking risks is a lot trickier.

Relativity and reference points

It's all relative.

Risk is not evaluated in a vacuum. It depends on our current context and situation. Whatever we currently experience and are used to is called our "adaptation level."

Something which we consistently experience becomes the new normal, and we use it as the reference point from which decisions are made.

Imagine, for example, you are a rich person—living in mansions and flying around on private jets. While walking along a park path you spot a hundred-dollar bill fluttering on the other side of a creek running through a steep ravine. Would you take the effort to retrieve it? Chances are the answer is no. The amount of benefit involved compared to the effort it would take is simply not worth it. Your life would not be materially changed if you acquired the extra money.

However, a suitcase full of hundred-dollar bills might interest you under the same circumstances. So would an investment opportunity that might potentially double your wealth.

There is a diminishing sensitivity to potential gains and losses. They are experienced not in the absolute, but as a proportion to what we currently have.

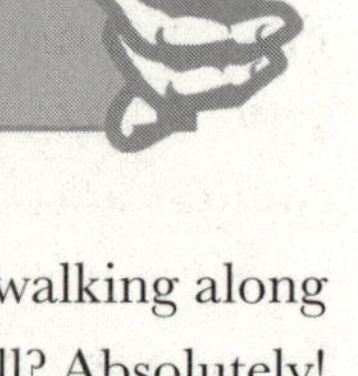

Now imagine you are homeless, destitute, cold, hungry, and walking along the same path. Would you choose to get the hundred-dollar bill? Absolutely! The money represents food, and a shower, and a warm blanket, which would considerably improve your current situation.

Yet the objective value of the money has not changed, and is the same for you in either situation. It is the potential benefit that has changed, given your current circumstances as the reference point.

The prevalence of the reward in your environment, and the ease with which you can access it, determines how much you value it, and how much you are willing to risk in its pursuit.

Let's do another thought experiment. Imagine you could spin a wheel and get a variety of outcomes. Each of the outcomes is positive and beneficial, except for one. That outcome has no value and no effect on you. We can call this the "good" wheel. If you spun the wheel and landed on the no-effect portion, you would consider it a "loss." You would be lamenting not getting the other potential gains that were available in that context.

Now imagine that there is a similar wheel, but the outcomes on it are all negative except for the same chance of getting the no-effect result. We can call this the "bad" wheel. If you spun the wheel and landed on the no-effect, you would feel relief and consider it a "win," since you dodged many potentially bad outcomes.

Yet the no-effect value on both wheels is exactly the same.

The positive or negative valuation of an outcome is heavily dependent on our current context.

This sometimes comes into play even when we don't get the outcome we want. If the outcome is a "near miss" that almost achieved our goal, we are more likely to continue to invest energy in pursuing it. In other words, the dopamine payoff of a near miss is sometimes as strong as an actual win.

For example, if a horse which you bet to win a race comes in second, you are more likely to bet on it again in the future, because you think you got very close to a win. Slot machines in casinos are carefully designed to disproportionately show near misses (two out of three matches on the win line). This keeps people in their chairs and feeding more money into the one-armed bandit.

Near misses provide powerful motivation to continue to seek a reward.

Loss aversion

Let's flip a coin in a typical "double or nothing" bet. If the coin comes up heads, you get double the amount which you bet. If tails, you will lose your bet. Economically, this proposition has a neutral value. Yet, most people would not take this bet because they are more focused on the possibility of the loss.

Losses loom larger than gains because we prioritize survival threats ahead of opportunities.

Imagine if you did not deal with an emergency as it was unfolding. The very meaning of the word implies that you have to pay attention to it, because it is important and needs your immediate attention. Your ancestors had a better chance to survive and reproduce if they prioritized negative threats.

There is a bowl of yummy ice cream on the table within reach of your spoon. Nearby someone is waiting to hit your hand with a claw hammer as soon as you try to reach for it. Do you keep reaching for the ice cream to get a taste, or do you figure out how to neutralize the possibility of getting whacked with the hammer first? The answer is pretty obvious—unless you really love your ice cream... Most of us can reliably delay gratification to deal with immediate threats.

A bird in the hand is worth two in the bush.

The saying above is absolutely correct. Giving up the one bird "sure thing" would require a counterbalancing opportunity to get two birds in exchange. This asymmetry varies based on the exact circumstances, but has been measured to be in the range of 1.5 to 2.5. Feel free to keep using the two-to-one ratio as a pretty good approximation. But keep in mind there is also a wide variation in loss aversion across individuals and circumstances.

Sure things and surprises

The primal brain likes sure things. It does not like to struggle with deciding among subtly different choices, and prefers obvious contrast.

Sure gains and sure losses are evaluated automatically by your primal brain.

One of the key functions of dopamine is to build a model of the world from our experiences. Events that fit our mental model of the world give us a sense of predictability. Dopamine is metered out to keep us motivated and moving towards our goals. If something unexpected happens, we need to pay extra attention. Since we did not anticipate it in our mental model it may be new and potentially important.

Unpredictable rewards are much more exciting than ones that can be predicted in advance.

The dopamine activation from unexpected events can be three to four times higher than from predictable ones!

However, there is a difference between unpredictability and randomness.

Our brain automatically tries to create and enforce patterns, and gets in trouble when truly random events are involved.

If I flipped a coin five times in a row and it came up heads each time, you would begin to suspect I was a cheat. In reality, we can expect this to happen about 3% of the time due to statistics. Even though each coin flip is random and independent of the others, our mind desperately wants to tease out the pattern, even if there is none…

This tendency to believe we can predict or control random events is amplified when we are active participants in the process. Even in purely random games of chance, direct involvement makes us feel like we have a better chance of getting a good outcome. Think about personally rolling the dice at a craps table, or selecting the numbers on a lottery ticket. Don't you feel more likely to win?

When we encounter near-miss outcomes we get more pleasure if we were actively involved. This may be partially due to the ownership effect, which we will explore later. Ownership, via possession, experience, or active participation, makes us overvalue the result.

Active participation in a random event makes us mistakenly believe that we can bend the outcome in our favor.

Chapter 9
THE EMOTIONAL LIFE

Embodied emotions

Emotions are a critical part of how we operate in the world. They are central to our decision making.

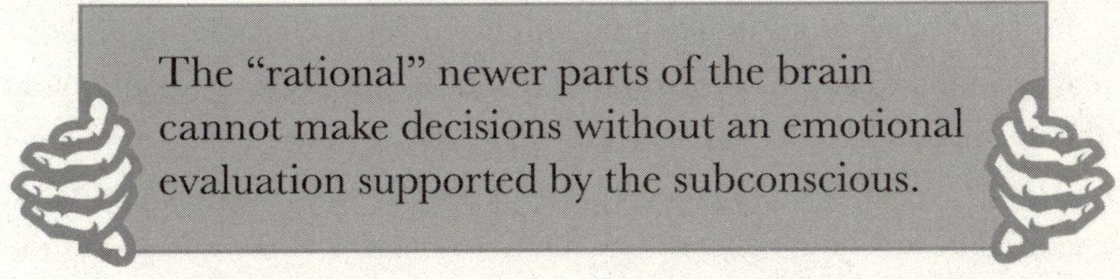

Even though I am skipping ahead, I will describe some of the key concepts related to emotions in the full context of evolution.

The key components of emotional experience are:

- An external stimulus—something which reaches us through our senses
- Past experience—the sum total of what brought us to this moment
- Mental images within the brain—concepts and simulations which are activated
- The evoked response in the body

To get an emotional reaction we usually have to detect a change in the environment. The change may be something obvious and overt, like a charging predator. Or it could be something as subtle as a momentary micro-emotion that flits across the face of a friend during a conversation.

Imagine a long-forgotten song, the smell of stale sweat in a gym locker room, or stepping foot into our childhood home after a long absence. Each of these events can start a powerful cascade inside the body.

Sometimes the response is direct and automatic. We jump backward from a branch in our path because we associate it with a snake. This happens preconsciously—even before we recognize the actual object.

Personal life experiences

Emotional processing can be very complex and deliberate.

Imagine being at a business function when you see a close friend deep in conversation with your sworn enemy. What are they talking about? What is the meaning of the interaction? How do existing power alliances change as a result? What new social risks or opportunities does this interaction portend? The meaning depends on your personal past experiences with the people involved, and their relationships with each other.

> Outside events are detected by the senses and processed through the total of our past experiences in automatic or nuanced ways.

The history of each individual is intensely personal. For example, I am not a big fan of needles, or even seeing them on TV. This is a result of almost passing out during my senior year high school blood drive donation. My association with needles is one of anxiety, fear, and pain. So, I prefer to close my eyes when blood needs to be drawn.

Another person may come from a long line of phlebotomists. They may associate drawing blood with proud feelings of professional competence in the delivery of quality health care.

Cultural overlays and interpretation

Our reactions to events are heavily dependent on the associations that we have with certain objects, symbols, or ideas.

Imagine a native of North America in the early 1500s. He comes across two crisscrossed sticks tied together with twine and stuck into the ground near a patch of some freshly turned earth. To such a person, it would most likely be a curiosity to be investigated.

But to the Catholic priest who comes across this same object, a massive edifice of meaning is triggered. He thinks about the religious cross and the multilayered meanings associated with this symbol. He may access memories about what put him on his religious path, and resulted from years of devoted service. He will feel empathy, veneration, and a sense of being in a sacred place. He might even be compelled to intone prayers over the unexpected grave of a rare fellow Christian in the New World.

The combination of the event and our associations is stored as an immediate feeling-state across our brain and body.

The event evokes an associated response which we call an emotion. This involves a variety of brain areas and the body as well. Body responses may include changes in heart rate, the degree of alertness, muscle tone, sweating, and tension in the pit of the stomach. Remember, there is no separation of the brain and other body systems. Our whole organism is responding to the event.

This direction is also two-way. It has long been known that certain body practices rewire our nervous systems and influence how we respond to events. Engaging in yoga, tai chi, meditation, or prayer can change our emotional states profoundly. We also know that restricting body movements also restricts emotions. Killing nerve cells in the face with Botox injections keeps your muscles from forming some facial expressions. This deadens your own experience of emotions in yourself and other people. Feeling emotions and moving our muscles are directly linked.

There are seven basic emotions which have been identified across all human cultures. These can be considered a universal alphabet as expressed in our facial expressions and gestures.

The universal human emotions include surprise, anger, fear, disgust, sadness, contempt, and joy.

We are faced with a nearly infinite choice of actions in any situation. If we were to catalog each possibility and deliberate about exactly how to proceed, we could not function. The body response immediately narrows our choices.

Responses can then be sorted by our "gut" to drop some from subsequent consideration. This allows us to decide, and react quickly to unfolding events. And to be clear—we never override or ignore these emotional signals. In the instances when we seem to use the "rational" mind, we are actually getting a body signal to focus on the long-term rather than the short-term.

The primary purpose of our embodied emotional response is to quickly narrow our choice of subsequent actions.

Chapter 10
SAFER IN THE HERD

Pluses and minuses of herds

The reptile brain is not very concerned with relationships. It's a finely tuned vehicle for individual survival. Breathe, eat, screw, fight, and run or slither away from danger. If you do all those things well enough, you will have more offspring, who can do more of the same.

For mammals, life is a team sport.

Mammals may be individually weaker, yet have a longer life expectancy than most earlier animals. Their babies have a much higher rate of survival. The ability to learn from experience and to cooperate gives the herd a collective edge.

There are many advantages to living in cooperative groups:

- Ability to rest and recover while remaining alert for danger
- Cooperation in acquiring food
- Sharing of food procured by the most able group members
- Organizing group defense against outside aggression

But such groups also introduce new problems:

- How to keep individuals from wandering off by themselves
- How to nurture the young through a long period of helplessness
- How to tell friend from foe
- How to create cooperation to accomplish group goals
- How to organize the group

Let's investigate the basic mechanisms by which mammals learned to function.

Isolation equals death

Herd animals monitor the location of other members of their tribe on an ongoing basis. When they cannot see any, their cortisol rises. When they return to the safety of the group, they are rewarded with the flow of oxytocin.

Want to keep a mammal from wandering off from the group? Make it feel pain every time this happens!

Emotional pain activates a significant portion of the physical pain pathways. It is not just something "in your head," but a survival adaptation. It gives you an immediate reason to rejoin the group, repair broken relationships, or reconsider the risks of operating alone. This improves your chances of survival.

Healthy social connections are not a bonus of some sort, but rather an essential part of mammalian well-being.

Social isolation is just as damaging to human life expectancy as a two-pack-per-day cigarette habit. The end of a deep relationship or the death of a close person is a major risk factor for anxiety or depression.

Even milder social events such as exclusion from the group or broken social alliances result in significant distress. They result in activations of areas that process pain—the dorsal anterior cingulate cortex and the insula.

Being accepted and included is a survival imperative for the mammalian brain.

The more you feel excluded, the more this is woven into the fabric of your being. This is especially striking when children experience rejection or abuse. Instead of a sense of safety, these early experiences lock them into feeling separate and afraid. The result is a broken attachment mechanism and lifelong negative mental health consequences.

Attachment and affection

A key issue for mammals is creating a powerful connection between children and caregivers.

A baby mammal is born helpless. It is completely dependent on continuous care by adults for its successful growth and development.

The most important driver of a baby mammal is the need for affection and the feeling of being loved.

Successful attachment is expressed by cuddling, vocalizations, grooming, and other stimulating contact. It is more important than other needs such as getting food and water. Without effective attachment, all the other needs will be ignored and the baby mammal will die.

For attachment to work, there has to be a reciprocal desire to take care of the baby by an adult (often and most centrally its mother). The septal area of the brain shifts the balance of our approach and avoidance tendencies. This area is rich in oxytocin receptors. If another animal was a hot mess of distress, incessantly crying and repeating frustrating behaviors, we would normally try to avoid it. But most mammal mothers voluntarily step into this role with their young under the influence of oxytocin.

Oxytocin kicks in during birth to facilitate labor, and also jumpstarts milk production. However, its longer-lasting effects are on the mother's willingness to care for her young. It is an all-in-one chemical that influences the body to give birth, create a food supply, and instill a long-lasting desire to nurture.

If the septal area is damaged, the mother may show less interest in caring for the child, and may even abandon it. The child grows up less securely attached and less able to care for its future children. If the parent provides attentive parenting, its children will have a higher density of oxytocin receptors in the septal area. This will make them, in turn, better parents to the next generation.

Avoidance and approach

Eventually as mammal babies grow up, they transfer their maternal attachments to the larger group on which they will depend. At this stage, things get a lot trickier than in the mother-child relationship. Suddenly, they have to decide and identify who are allies and supporters, versus outsiders who mean them harm.

The multitasking oxytocin steps in again. Far from being the "cuddle drug," it also has a dark side.

Mammals will act with aggression against disliked and threatening outsiders.

We can tell at a glance whether a stranger is socially dominant, and how trustworthy they are. The loving mother is tender and caring with her child. But she will spring into action and ferociously defend it against all hostile strangers. It is not only the mothers who are on alert for threats. All outsiders are seen as likely threats and handled with suspicion and aggression by members of the group.

The effects of oxytocin are different in primates. People in particular seem to naturally divide others into one of three categories: the liked ingroup, the disliked outgroup, and unknown strangers. If we meet such strangers in a safe and supportive environment where oxytocin is flowing, we will be more likely to give them the benefit of the doubt.

People will sometimes accept unknown strangers into their trusted ingroup.

There is a part of the brain that helps specifically with the recognition of allies. The *fusiform face area* (FFA) operates separately from our general object-recognition system. It works more quickly and helps us to recognize others. We can only do this with right-side-up faces. Some arboreal monkeys, which often hang upside-down by their tails, can recognize faces in any orientation. Once we recognize a particular friend, we process the situation through the *medial prefrontal cortex*—a part of the brain that regulates social behavior. We pay more attention to close friends. Strangers' faces do not light up this brain area.

People with various degrees of autism do not activate the FFA when looking at others. Instead, they use the *inferior temporal gyrus*—an area of the brain which is normally used to process complex visual scenes. In effect they do not see a wholistic face and associate it with a known person. They process the individual features of the face as disconnected objects, without the ability to read unified facial expressions. They visually reconstruct faces with the same detachment as inanimate objects. Because of this, they cannot glean all of the rich emotional information available to others.

We have evolved to recognize and respond to the faces of friends.

Status and dominance

Mammals band together to get the advantages of cooperation, and to present a united front to the outside world. But within the group itself it is a very different story. Individuals are always jockeying for position. Respect and dominance feel good, low status feels awful. Unless you are the leader, you are constantly accommodating the needs of others.

Top ranking individuals, either males or females depending on the mammal species, get the many benefits of high status.

These benefits include eating first, getting the best food, and support from strong social alliances. They extend to more frequent mating opportunities with higher status partners, and access to the best care for their offspring. When you become a dominant mammal and gain power, your testosterone rises and cortisol levels drop. You feel confident, assertive, and comfortable.

If you have a low status within the group, life is very different. You are the last to eat and often go hungry. You are less physically safe since you are on the outskirts of the group and isolated. You also get fewer mating opportunities—sometimes none at all. Your genes are screaming for you to do something about this awful situation, and drive you via cortisol spikes to act. When all your choices are bad, you become more desperate, and are willing to take greater risks to improve your situation.

As you can see from these starkly different outcomes, dominance is worth fighting for and investing in. High-status individuals will struggle to maintain their positions. Low-status individuals will do the same to improve theirs. The battle for king of the hill never ends.

Every mammal feels stress when it sees threats to its social bonds or position.

Bigger brains allow us to continuously update information about our status within the group, as well as that of others. The larger a mammal's brain, the more social information it can process and update. Larger brain sizes in people and other primates allow for the formation of complex social structures and larger tribes.

Mammals cannot easily carry extra food or other survival necessities. So, they invest all of their spare energy into building and maintaining social alliances which can be called upon in times of need.

Mammals are always comparing their situation to others' and investing in activities to improve their standing in the group.

Chapter 11
GOOD NIGHT, SWEET DREAMS

The universal need for sleep

Our perception of the world is waking-biased.

Most of the interesting and complex behaviors in life seem to happen when we are awake. At best, many people think of sleep as being a necessary and unproductive evil. They tolerate it so they can get back to busy lives and the flickering screens in front of them.

In reality, sleep is fundamental to most animal and insect life on earth. Almost every animal species sleeps. Only regular rest, repair, and maintenance can support life. You get all this, and more, during sleep.

Sleep is the original state of life from which wakefulness emerged.

Sleep is an absolute necessity to staying healthy and fighting off death for as long as possible. The more complex the brain and nervous system, the more demands are placed on sleep to support optimal functioning.

Sleep seems to be a waste of time, or even dangerous. Our brain could be fighting off enemies, finding food, or looking for mating opportunities instead. But because of our complex bodies and brains, sleep is critical for clean-up, maintenance, and integration of each day's experiences. This maintenance applies not only to the individual, but also to our ability to function in large cooperative groups.

There are three major types of sleep: deep sleep, NREM, and REM.

Deep sleep is mainly about cleaning out toxins and erasing information which no longer supports our survival. It is the earliest evolutionary development. During deep sleep we completely lose our sense of consciousness and perception of time. The whole cortex takes on a single slow-wave oscillating rhythm. Deep sleep is used to synchronize, repair, and weaken or remove unneeded connections. The waking brain is concerned with taking in and processing information in real time. In deep sleep, the brain turns inwards to trim the day's activities down to the essentials.

NREM (non-REM) sleep transfers the past day's short-term memories from the hippocampus to the more stable neocortex for long-term future retrieval.

REM (rapid eye movement) sleep developed later, and only in some more recent species like birds and mammals, to carry out new functions.

As we will soon explore, the voluntary muscles of the body are paralyzed during REM sleep. REM is relatively easy to accomplish when you are resting on the ground. But it was so critical that specialized responses were created in some animals. For example, some migratory birds take tiny REM micro-naps short enough to keep them from falling out of the sky. Similarly, certain species of aquatic mammals like dolphins alternate REM sleep between their right and left hemispheres. This keeps them from drowning—allowing them to consciously surface and breathe while part of their brain is sleeping.

Deep sleep is front-loaded earlier in the night and used mainly to prune out unnecessary neural connections. NREM then moves memories from short-term storage into long-term. Tail-weighted REM sleep is used to strengthen certain connections. It overlays that day's impressions onto the lifetime of valuable prior experience, and consolidates them for future use.

Human sleep

Normal human sleep is approximately seven to eight hours during the night. It is also followed by a thirty- to sixty-minute nap in the afternoon. This is independent of geography or culture. We experience a dip in our alertness and sleep pressure in the mid-afternoon, whether we choose to recognize and honor the need or not.

The first evolutionary step of modern humans was to come down from the relative safety of the trees on the African savannah. Since life on the ground was a lot more dangerous, there was significant pressure to spend less time sleeping.

We spend approximately 8 hours sleeping, compared to 10 to 15 hours among our primate cousins.

What allowed for shorter sleep is most likely our cultural taming of fire, and gathering in larger tribal groups. Fire scared off and kept large predators at bay. It also provided a natural fumigation since the smoke kept insects from biting us. A few weary lookouts most likely completed this ancient scene, as they kept a watchful eye over the rest of the sleeping group.

To compensate for the massive decrease in sleep time, humans evolved to have a more intense form of sleep, heavily favoring dreaming and REM.

Between a fourth and a fifth of a normal night's sleep is devoted to REM. This is in sharp contrast to an average of 9% for other primates. There are no other species that have this massive proportion of REM sleep.

REM is critical for maintaining emotional calibration and supporting appropriate social behaviors.

Without adequate REM we can't gauge facial expressions or body gestures accurately. We assume the worst about people's intentions and motivations, and are more likely to perceive them as a threat. We also can't regulate our emotional reactions and respond in a nuanced way to others. Our emotional health is the basis of our ability to create large, stable, and bonded groups. This, in turn, is the prerequisite for forming our sophisticated societies. Civilization and successful cooperation are built on consistent and adequate REM sleep.

The effects of not sleeping

Two important mechanisms govern our sleep.

Sleep pressure is a combination of cycling daily rhythms and a running clock of how long we have been awake.

Most of us are familiar with the circadian twenty-four-hour rhythm. It leads to cyclical drowsiness during the evening and night hours. Think of this as a slow-moving wave that repeats every day. The circadian rhythm creates alertness, or pulls you towards drowsiness based on the amount of light in your environment. In the natural world, this light and dark pattern was a very consistent experience. Unfortunately, we have largely destroyed the reliability of it with the presence of artificial lights. And we willfully ignore it with devastating consequences.

A second sleep mechanism acts like an ongoing sleep pressure clock that measures how long we have been awake. This timer is only reset after a significant sleep event.

Our livers continuously produce a substance called *adenosine* while we are awake. It circulates in the whole body and continues to increase inside of cells. When it binds to adenosine receptors, it exerts a powerful and increasing pressure to get rest. Substances like caffeine bind to the same receptors and block the effects of adenosine.

Caffeine is not a stimulant which makes you more alert. It temporarily masks the sleep pressure building up inside of your body after long periods of wakefulness.

With adequate sleep, our brain supports our ability to learn, make effective decisions, improve physical skills, and consolidate new memories. It also helps us to make sense of our emotional inner world and prepares us for the nuanced social interactions required the next day.

After sixteen hours of being awake, the brain starts to catastrophically break down.

We start relying on the more primitive parts of the brain. Normally there is a strong link between the amygdala and the prefrontal cortex. The amygdala governs strong emotions, and the cortex can exert some degree of control and executive function to override it. Think of it as a feedback loop and a self-regulating system. Lack of sleep breaks this connection.

Without sleep, the brain swings wildly between positive and negative emotional extremes.

Nuanced responses and self-regulation become impossible in many circumstances. During sleep deprivation, and for some time after, our body is stuck in fight-flight-freeze mode. It is operating on a primitive survival-mode autopilot.

How important is sleep to our mental well-being?

Consider the following:

- Sleep disturbances are strongly associated with substance abuse and addiction
- Chances of drug-use relapse are much higher when we can't self-regulate

- Every major psychiatric condition involves dysregulated sleep
- If you don't get proper sleep on the very first night after learning, you will never consolidate the information, regardless of any subsequent "catch-up sleep"

And it is not just the brain that suffers because of inadequate sleep. You are much more likely to get into a car accident if you are tired. Lack of sleep is a bigger contributor to accidents than driving while impaired. Accidents are forty times more likely when you are both tired and impaired! You are also much more likely to die of many cancers, and to suffer strokes and heart attacks.

And you can't compensate for this by taking sleeping pills. Such remedies only "knock you out" by paralyzing your voluntary muscles.

Sleeping pills provide none of the restorative benefits of sleep.

You are also weakening your immune system. Sleep deprivation makes you much more susceptible to various bacterial and viral infections. It also prolongs recovery time from injuries. When you get sick, your immune system increases the sleep pressure to force bed rest and facilitate recovery.

Regular and adequate natural sleep is essential daily life support.

REM sleep

Human sleep proceeds in approximately 90-minute cycles. During each cycle we drop down into deep sleep, followed by NREM, and REM. Think of it as a washing machine. The first part of the cycle washes away the clutter and dirt with detergent. The second part is like a color-brightening additive which reinforces and supports key new information. The third part fuses the new additives permanently into place with the existing fabric of our past experiences.

Not only is REM sleep at the end of each sleep cycle, but it is also more heavily weighted as the night progresses. Each consecutive sleep cycle has a higher percentage of REM. The last cycle is the one with the most.

When we sleep less than six hours, we are losing a big chunk of our REM processing time for the night.

Brain scans show stronger-than-normal activation in the visual, motor, emotional, and memory regions. The visuospatial regions in the back of the brain process complex visual information. The motor cortex normally initiates movement. But as you will see in the next section, while this area is active, all voluntary movement control is cut off—leaving us paralyzed.

The amygdala and cingulate cortex are also highly active—generating and processing emotions. Finally, the hippocampus and adjacent areas are busy processing autobiographical memories. The areas mentioned above are actually up to a third more active than when we are awake! At the same time, there is a deactivation in the parts which control rational logical thinking. Put all this together and what you get is a simulation engine.

REM dreaming is a mashup of vivid emotional experiences from the previous day and wild, uncontrolled storylines unconstrained by realism.

About a third to half of our dreaming themes are directly tied to events that we experienced during the day. They focus on subjects of emotional concern to us. This memory replay happens during REM sleep much slower than in real life—possibly down to half or quarter speed. The slow replay gives us time to process and integrate all of the available information. This also explains why our subjective plot duration in dreams often seems to last much longer than time passing in the real world.

The previous day's information is effectively processed and combined with our past life experience. This forms a stable and coherent updated model of the world. We connect the new events to each other, and also combine them with our previous experiences.

At the same time, the strong emotions which accompanied the day's events can be jettisoned because they are no longer useful. Imagine you had accidentally burned your hand on a hot stove. The vivid event would need to be remembered in the future—including what led up to it. However, you do not want to re-experience the trauma at its original intensity every time you bring up the memory again.

REM sleep acts as a gentle therapy—separating the information which needs to be remembered from the original highly emotional context.

If this process is disrupted, the traumatic reenactment of the memory will continue to happen. This is commonly seen among people who have experienced post-traumatic stress disorder (PTSD). Not coincidentally, they are more likely to be unable to get a good night's sleep after such traumatic events.

REM sleep recalibrates our ability to accurately read the facial expressions of others.

Without sleep, our impressions of other people become distorted. We assume that they mean us harm, or are negatively predisposed towards us. REM sleep allows us to re-tune every night so we are ready to navigate our social worlds accurately, and to respond appropriately. The more REM sleep we get, the better our ability to do this becomes. With short sleep we experience the world as a threatening place, and default to a fear bias. This emotional recalibration ability comes online before our transition into adolescence. It is when we start paying particular attention to the behavior of our peers.

Dreams as a rehearsal for dangerous events

The brain consolidates each day's new and interesting events into long-term memories. It also throws away information that is no longer needed.

But there is another vital reason we spend a considerable portion of our lives asleep. The fact that the brain turns off voluntary motor control during REM gives us a hint about another critical sleep purpose.

Simulating dangerous activities during sleep prepares us without paying the high price of failing in real life.

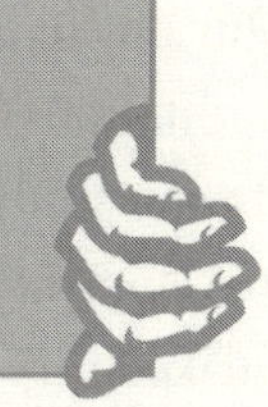

The nighttime dream world is often a literal nightmare of fight-or-flight scenarios which recur over and over. You are the star of this absurd cavalcade of experiences. Many dreams involve physical and emotional dangers, and your attempts to deal with them. You are bathed in fear and anger and experience massive stress. Across all cultures, the most common dreams are about being attacked or chased. Other universal topics include drowning, being lost or trapped, being sick or dying, getting injured, being naked in public (and other social threats), or being caught in some kind of natural or man-made disaster.

The dream world is frequently populated with a wide variety of terrifying circumstances that we are forced to confront.

We run, or fight, or struggle to try to deal with the situations. There is no way for our brain to know that dreams are not real. That's the whole point.

By paralyzing our bodies, we are safe to practice dangerous physical events during REM sleep.

Our brain completely disconnects our voluntary muscles during these simulations. This ensures that the imaginary bear in our dream does not chase us off of a real cliff by accident while we are asleep. The worst that will happen to us after these life-or-death struggles is to startle ourselves awake and sit bolt upright in a pool of sweat.

Of course, all of the involuntary muscles necessary to keep us alive continue to function during REM. This includes breathing and circulation.

People are really good at voluntary simulation while awake. It has been shown that visualizing successful basketball free-throws improves performance as much as actual practice. The brain provides us with forced simulation training for high-stakes survival events every single night of our lives. This allows us to safely try out innovative problem-solving approaches.

Remembering, learning, and creativity

Sleep is critical for the learning and consolidation of new factual information.

If you don't sleep well on the night after learning, you lose the ability to consolidate the memory.

Immediate sleep is required, and no amount of subsequent sleep on the following nights will help. Sleep is what keeps you from forgetting. Extra time spent awake beyond a normal day results in a faster decay of memories.

The reason is simple. Factual info is stored daily in the hippocampus. After a night of proper sleep, it is moved and properly integrated with the existing information in the neocortex. This is a much more stable place for the subsequent recall. The transfer work happens primarily during the non-REM (NREM) portions of each sleep cycle.

A proper night's sleep flushes out short-term memories to make room for new ones, and saves important ones into your long-term storage.

When you wake up, you are ready to learn new information and have key facts safely tucked away for future use. You may also have access to memories which you were unable to recall the day before.

There is also strong evidence that we can selectively assist which facts will be most strongly consolidated at night. Sleep is an intelligent process that picks and chooses which memories to pay attention to. This is partly based on how we encoded them during the learning process.

The consolidation of new physical skills also happens during sleep. After proper REM, our skills become more automatic and improve in terms of both speed and accuracy. REM is tail weighted over the course of the night. Robbing yourself of the last ninety-minute sleep cycle will undo much of the benefit of previous physical practice.

Another vital function of sleep is to integrate new information with the accumulated impressions of our whole lives to date. In other words, new connections are formed or strengthened among brain areas. The REM brain is busy building non-obvious and distant connections by default.

REM sleep nurtures creativity and allows us to get novel insights to solve problems.

Chapter 12
MONKEY SEE, MONKEY DO

Mirror neurons

In monkeys and other higher primates, a strange fact was discovered. The premotor area in the brain (also known as F5) lights up when monkeys carry out certain gestures. But it also lights up when the monkeys see another animal doing the same motions. The observer's brain acts as if it was performing the gesture at the same time as the animal being observed.

> Mirror neurons fire when we move our bodies, and also when we observe others doing the same actions. Doing and seeing are unified.

The *classical mirroring* system fires both when you lift your finger and when you see someone else do it. However, we don't want to be forced to copy the gestures and actions of everyone around us. The inhibitory *super mirroring* system stops us when watching others. But it is not active when we initiate our own voluntary movements.

Mirror neurons exist throughout the brain and function in a variety of ways. Some fire only for certain gestures or movements. Others fire when watching a video of another moving. Still others only respond to live animals nearby. Some only fire when the action is hidden from view—reacting as if they could imagine what was going on. Certain mirror neurons are tuned towards a specific goal or reward. For example, specialized mirror neurons fire only when you are eating an object, rather than simply moving it from place to place.

Imitation

The reptile's world is fairly simple. When meeting another animal, a lizard has to decide whether it's food, represents a threat, or might be a potential mate. But mammals have to make much more nuanced distinctions, and also to cooperate.

Many other animals have complex vocalizations and their own languages. However, these often serve very basic ends, such as attracting mates or scaring away potential threats. Mammals are much more sophisticated. They recognize specific individuals within their group and know their place in the social hierarchy. They use this information to navigate ever-changing alliances.

How can mammals cooperate if they can't speak using complex verbal languages?

The key is body language. Mammals can detect the slightest changes in facial expressions and postures. This is a treasure trove of information. Even for modern humans it has been shown that the words we say play only a minor role in what we communicate. More is conveyed by our tone of voice. But the majority of information comes in through body language.

The earliest modern humans have existed for at least 200,000 years. Yet evidence of culture such as art, religion, language, and complex tools first emerged around 50,000 years ago. In the intervening period our species advanced by imitation. Minor improvements in shelter building, tool creation, and hunting tactics could be passed from one individual to another. This continued across many generations as we imitated each other. A virtuous feedback loop of learned culture brought us to where we are today.

Even the extended period of helplessness in human children offers many evolutionary advantages. To a parent, it often seems that babies are pooping, crying, or eating all of the time. Young children are actually keenly observing and internally imitating the adults around them. Since there is much to learn from their surrounding tribe, observation provides a powerful advantage later in life.

Getting into other people's heads

The entry point into someone else's head is mirroring. We do not have to imagine what they are feeling. By mirroring their actions, we can directly replicate their mental state inside of our brains. This amazing ability to read minds operates all the time, even when we are not consciously trying to understand another's thought process.

The mirroring system automatically processes visual information and models another's actions.

But just watching action is not enough. We have to simulate what is going on in another person's head to understand and assign meaning to the actions.

As developing children, we get to a point when we realize that other people behave differently from us for their own reasons, and view life from their unique perspectives. This critical development is called the *theory of mind* by psychologists. In other words, we eventually understand that we need to develop a model of what is inside of other people's heads. Once we do, we can navigate our social dynamics with them.

Understanding another's thoughts and motivations is called mentalizing. It involves simulating another person's responses based on our available knowledge about them.

As mammals, we need to be able to operate effectively within our group. Being able to predict the thoughts of those around us is critical to our survival. We have to be able to anticipate their reactions to a course of action we are considering. Since these reactions are not automatic, they require effort to predict.

Grabbing food from the boss at a company event would evoke a different reaction than grabbing it off of your close friend's plate with a smile on your face. We need to be able to predict the chain of resulting consequences depending on the context and the people involved.

Imagining the reactions of specific people allows us to increase social rewards and minimize social pain.

Mentalizing works not only for unfolding events, but also to predict the future full of shifting social alliances.

Social thinking and mentalizing is a critical ability, and has dedicated systems in the brain. While mentalizing is going on, other brain systems involving fluid intelligence, non-social reasoning, and working memory are deactivated. Unlike simple mirroring of physical actions, mentalizing can be thrown off track or shut down if we are distracted or focused on another conscious reasoning task.

We can think about social relationships or abstract concepts—but not both simultaneously.

Social thinking is not something that we only do consciously. It literally takes up every spare moment—both when we are awake and asleep. When our minds are not immediately occupied by conscious thoughts, they do not go dormant. Instead, we go back to simulating social scenarios—trying to gain a survival advantage in our future interactions with others. Similar regions of the brain also light up while we are dreaming during REM sleep.

Our mind defaults to social thinking automatically—priming us to see the world in terms of other people's perspectives.

Empathy and sympathy

Accurately modeling and predicting others' behavior is very hard work. So, our energy-miser brain often takes a shortcut. We tend to imagine other people are like us—they would act like us, think like us, and like the same things as us. In effect we practice the Golden Rule—treat others as you want to be treated.

To go beyond this limitation, we have to engage the theory of mind. We understand that what other people believe and want is different from our desires and goals.

To be empathetic requires three distinct processes to come together:

- **Mind reading**—mirroring and mentalizing to understand what another is thinking
- **Affect matching**—synchronizing your mental state and outward actions and gestures with theirs
- **Empathic motivation**—proactively wanting to help the person with little regard to your own needs

If the chain is broken at any point, empathetic behavior will not occur.

For example, when we see someone else's facial expression, our face immediately shifts into a subtly similar configuration. But if a person is unable to mimic, they do not read the emotions of others well. This can happen due to a stroke, or by voluntarily paralyzing the nerves of the face with Botox injections.

During affect matching, we may activate the pain distress network housed in the anterior insula and dorsal anterior cingulate cortex areas. This can even happen when we are reading about a painful event that happens to others.

When we see a close person in pain, we experience the pain as if it was happening to us.

Even though we feel another's pain, the response may not always be a motivation to help. Most people feel empathetic when bad things happen to good people or those who are helpless.

However, if someone is perceived to be doing wrong, our response may shift and even vary by sex. In a certain social experiment, cheaters were given mild electric shocks as a punishment. Women who observed this still responded empathetically. The men not only had a lowered empathy response but activated their reward centers instead. They apparently experienced some pleasure at the just punishment of another. As you will see in later chapters about culture, we derive pleasure from enforcing the social rules and norms of our group.

During affect matching we may arrive at an avoidance behavior instead of the desire to help. Once we take on the emotions of another, we may feel so icky that we want to get out of the state as quickly as possible. As I also noted earlier, if the septal area is damaged, it is less able to take the converging inputs from other brain areas and turn them into helpful action.

PART III

CLUMSY BIGHEADS

Chapter 13
HUMBLE BEGINNINGS

Aren't we amazing?!

We can communicate with billions of people anywhere on the planet instantly. We fly through the skies at hundreds of miles per hour with all the drama of sitting in our living room recliners. We can hurl spacecraft out of Earth's gravitational well and across tens of billions of miles—beyond the outer reaches of the solar system. We can also incinerate millions of people in a nuclear fireball at the push of a button.

We must be the masters of space and time—secure in our unique place in the universe, and with dominion over all other life on the planet! We just popped into existence fully formed, without precedent, and qualitatively better than anything around us!

Time for a reality check…

Ancient people were slow, weak, tired easily, and were ineffectual predators. Poor eyesight, slow reflexes, and a crude sense of smell made them practically defenseless, especially at night. Even though they were omnivorous, our distant grandparents were definitely not at the top of the food chain. For over two million years they roamed the African plains afraid of being killed by apex predators.

They ate various plants, dug in the ground for larva and insects, and cornered an occasional small animal or bird. But hunting large game was a rare event, and when they did get their hands on some, it was most likely to be the carrion remains of another predator's kill.

Yes, the bigger brain helped a bit. But it was not a decisive advantage.

Early humans were marginal players on the world stage—surviving for a long time around the edges of more effective animal ecosystems.

Our ancestors' struggles and triumphs played out over long periods of time. The imprints of that environment are still with us today. We look for landscapes that offer good sightlines to spot dangers, as well as a refuge to escape from them. In landscape art we are drawn to the right mix or protection (trees to climb), fresh water (in the form of streams or lakeshores), and food (the biodiversity of mixed forest clearings). It seems that even our sense of aesthetics and beauty is tied to the environment that helped us to survive.

We need contact with nature in order to be in balance and to live healthy lives. Our urban environments place many stresses on us. *Nature deficit disorder* has come to be recognized as a medical issue. As little as 20-30 minutes per day in a natural environment has been shown to significantly lower cortisol levels.

The degree of walkability of urban neighborhoods is highly correlated with the average weight of the people who live in it. Our performance on cognitive tasks has shown to be better when we spend time in nature, including parks in urban areas. The bottom line is that landscapes like the ones we evolved in are healthier for our minds and bodies.

Other archaic humans

It would be wrong to assume modern people were the only viable branch of the human tree. Evolution continued to experiment and spread its bets. At least three strains of people migrated out of Africa at various times and even coexisted.

Our common ancestor Homo heidelbergensis ventured out of Africa between 500,000 and 600,000 years ago. One population spread into Europe and western Asia and became known as Neanderthals. The other went east into Asia and the Pacific and became known as Denisovans.

Some of the people who stayed in Africa had, by 250,000 years ago, become our direct ancestors Homo sapiens. Around 70,000 years ago, some of them also pushed out into Eurasia and encountered their ancient cousins. About 50,000 years ago Homo sapiens, Neanderthals, and Denisovans sometimes occupied the same habitats. They may have been on the verge of becoming different species.

By 30,000 years ago only Homo sapiens remained worldwide.

What happened to the Neanderthals and Denisovans?

Genes tell the story. Between one and four percent of uniquely human DNA in Europeans and Middle Easterners is from Neanderthals. Similarly, up to six percent of DNA from Pacific Islanders is from Denisovans, as is that of some aboriginal Australians.

None of the original East African populations show any evidence of Neanderthal or Denisovan DNA. There was no backward migration from the archaic human explorers into Africa. Homo sapiens spread across the whole globe. In various times and places, they encountered groupings of our ancient cousins. These were either killed off, outcompeted, or interbred out of existence.

The exodus of Homo sapiens out of Africa overlapped with and absorbed populations of more ancient humans spread out across the rest of Eurasia and the Pacific.

Brain drain

Primates such as lemurs were our common ancestors 65 million years ago. About 25 million years ago, apes split from monkeys. Between six and eight million years ago, humans also split from orangutans, gorillas, chimps, and pigmy chimps in that order.

We differ from other great apes in the ability to walk upright, and our larger brains.

Some draw an inevitable straight line between those differences and our current dominance of the planet. In reality, each of those evolutionary changes had significant tradeoffs.

Walking upright frees up our hands to carry objects, as well as craft and use tools. But it makes us weaker and slower because we can only use two out of four limbs for locomotion. It also puts a strain on our knees, hips, and spine because more load-bearing weight is concentrated there. The formerly strong shoulders atrophied into a weaker area as well. More strain was placed on our neck to balance and stabilize a larger head on a single central support. Our upright legacy gave us bad knees, painful backs and necks, and injury-prone shoulders.

Bigger brains allow us to learn from our environment and manage the complex relationships needed to maintain larger cooperative tribal groups. But they do so by extracting a crushing energy penalty.

Modern human brains require massive amounts of energy to operate.

Our brains are only about two to three percent of our body mass, but require between 25 and 35 percent of our resting energy to function. This is especially startling when compared to the eight percent average of other great ape brains.

All organisms need to balance competing needs. So how did early humans compensate for the voracious energy demands of their brains? As we have already seen, one adaptation was to have weaker physical bodies. This lowered the requirements for maintaining them. The other adaptation was to devote less time to finding and eating food.

Taming fire led to a cascade of events that allowed our brains to grow even bigger and more powerful.

Our direct ancestors Homo erectus as well as Neanderthals were using fire as part of their daily lives over 300,000 years ago.

The most important consequence of fire control was our ability to cook food.

Cooking had several important benefits for people:

- Killing dangerous germs and parasites—decreasing the risk of disease and death
- Increasing the range of foods which are edible—modern staples such as wheat and rice, as well as tubers like potatoes, were inedible prior to the advent of cooking
- Making it quicker to chew and ingest food—compare the single hour per day that people need to feed with the five hours spent by chimps, who need to chew all of their food in its raw state
- Pre-digesting food—requiring less work for our digestive systems to tap and release the full energy content of food

The evolutionary arms race had begun.

Cooked food allowed for shorter intestines and more efficient digestive systems. Our jaws would get smaller since our teeth did not need to do so much of the work of chewing. This evolution continues to this day, as anyone who has had their impacted wisdom teeth removed can attest.

A more efficient digestive system relying on cooked food directly led to the development of larger brains.

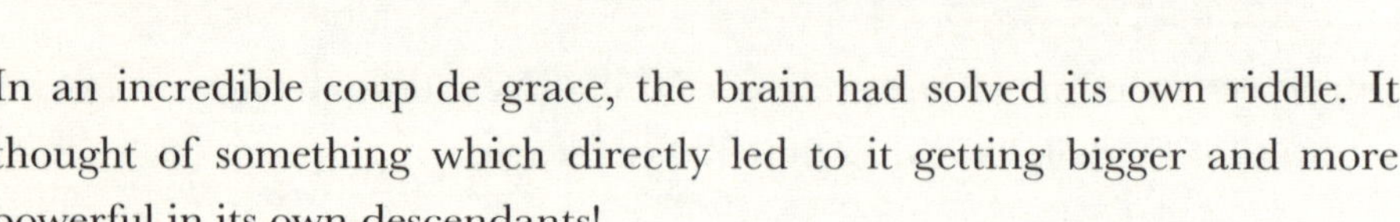

In an incredible coup de grace, the brain had solved its own riddle. It thought of something which directly led to it getting bigger and more powerful in its own descendants!

In the blink of the evolutionary eye, by 150,000 years ago, our fire-using East African ancestors came to be almost exactly like us. Complete with smaller jaws and giant brains, they jumped quickly to the top of the food chain. The world has never been the same.

Chapter 14
BIG BABIES

Big brains require big skulls.

Giving birth to big-skulled infants created its own set of problems:

- Dangers of childbirth for the mother
- Adaptations of the infant
- Extended period of helplessness and immaturity
- Greater investment in each child

Death by cannonball

I have known many women who have told scary tales of giving vaginal birth to massive babies. Thanks to modern medicine, the risks of the mother dying during delivery are very low. But this was not the case in the distant past. Women commonly died during the birth process. The fully dilated size of the cervical opening in the womb is 10 centimeters! Imagine pushing out a softball-sized head over hours or even days of active labor—a truly heroic feat…

One way of dealing with this is to forget the pain of childbirth afterward, so you would be willing to go through the experience again. The body's cannabinoid receptors are effectively integrated into a woman's reproductive system. Even though they do not dull the experience of pain, they do help to keep it from being remembered. During labor, levels of anandamide, the "bliss" endocannabinoid, quadruple and even help with contractions.

Babies not only have to pass through the womb and birth canal, but also through the bones of the pelvic girdle itself. Women's hips are relatively wide. Men look for these "childbearing hips" automatically. Across all cultures, a waist-to-hip ratio close to 0.7 is considered the most attractive. Men are, at a glance, selecting for mates who can successfully deliver a baby. But there is a practical limit to the width of the hips. Unlike other primates, women have a relatively thick pelvis to bear the weight of walking upright. This in turn makes the pelvic girdle narrower.

> Since death during childbirth of large babies was common, natural selection favored women who gave birth earlier.

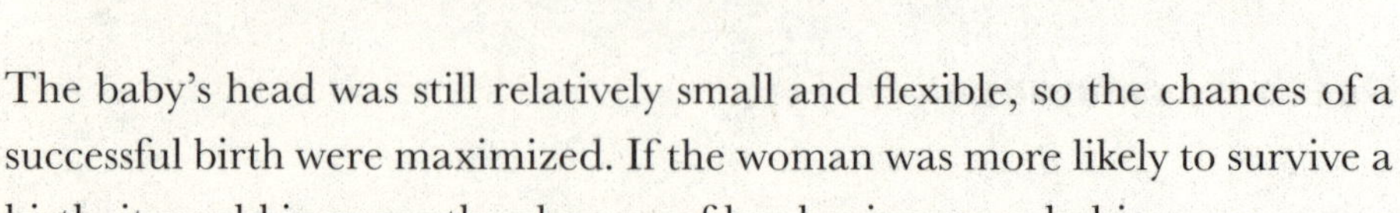

The baby's head was still relatively small and flexible, so the chances of a successful birth were maximized. If the woman was more likely to survive a birth, it would increase the chances of her having more babies.

Neonatal freaks

To deal with giant brains, human infants evolved some bizarre adaptations.

- **Multi-part skulls**—Newborns have a flexible skull configuration consisting of disconnected plates and soft tissue between them. Many babies have a big soft spot at the top of their heads (the fontanel) which may not close and fuse for as long as 18 months. The baby's head could be squeezed through the birth canal more easily, and allow the brain to grow quickly after birth before the skull fused.
- **Premature births**—The first three months after delivery are sometimes called the "fourth trimester." During this time, the baby often stays on the reverse night-day cycle that it maintained in the womb. It prefers to be tightly swaddled, to simulate the familiar environment inside of the tight uterus. The brain and vital body systems remain very underdeveloped during this time.
- **Rapid brain growth**—Chimps, our closest great ape cousins, are born with brains slightly less than half of their eventual adult size. In human infants, the brain is only a quarter of its adult size. Massive brain growth occurs until the age of five, and continues in a more measured way until the early twenties. Most of human brain development occurs outside the womb. This allows for much more adaptation to the environment at the level of the individual.

Helpless learners

A baby giraffe drops two meters to the ground…

It can stand within a half hour, and starts walking after another half hour passes.

Giraffes are a perfect example of *precocial* mammals. Such animals are relatively self-sufficient at birth. Chimp babies can clutch onto their mother within a day—a far cry from absolutely helpless human babies. People are the quintessential *altricial* animals. We are unable to move on our own and require intensive support long after birth.

Children depend on adults for many years to get food, comfort, protection, and social education.

It is not just the mother who takes care of the child. Active involvement from the whole group is required. As we explored earlier, isolation equals death for mammals. This is especially true for human babies. Successful attachment to the mother, and strong bonding with tribe members, is supported at a chemical level. This ensures that the child is cared for and nurtured.

The payoffs from this are powerful.

Human children can be educated and socialized to a far greater degree than the young of any other species.

While children are not a blank slate, they can be profoundly shaped by the surrounding environment and social forces.

Chapter 15
SEXY APES

Are we sluts?

Some people want to fill the world with silly love songs…

And they have. Over 90% of songs, consistently across all cultures and times, have to do with courtship or relationships. The centrality of this theme is not remarkable, since reproduction is the first imperative of all life. With a highly social species like humans, it is bound to occupy much of our time and attention.

But is the lifelong romantic pair bond the natural and desirable state of things? Do we meet, fall in love, and live happily ever after? Let's strip away the many layers of cultural and religious beliefs and look to underlying biology for clues.

Among mammals, only 3-5% of species are monogamous. Recent research suggests males will accept monogamy when they cannot dominate the females of their species. Another exception is when access to females is difficult. This can be because of population density or extended operating range. Under those conditions, the bachelor will place a more significant bet on having offspring with just one female. By contrast, over 90% of mammal species are highly promiscuous. Both males and females can have multiple sexual partners—sometimes even on the same day.

Our closest great ape cousins display a wide variety of mating strategies. Orangutans are a solitary species whose members get together occasionally for sex. But they do not form long-term bonds, and mothers raise the babies alone. Gorillas operate in groups dominated by a single alpha male. This "silverback" has an exclusive ability to mate with mature females in his harem. There is no real competition with other males to have sex, so a gorilla's balls are small and tucked inside of his body for protection.

Chimpanzees live in groups with multiple males and females, and are promiscuous. Genetic testing suggests that half of chimp babies are not being raised by their biological fathers. Male chimps take every opportunity to mate. Bonobos (also known as pygmy chimps) are highly promiscuous. They engage in sex as a way of cementing social alliances, as well as a substitute for aggression. Both chimps and bonobos have relatively large air-cooled testicles and are mating opportunists.

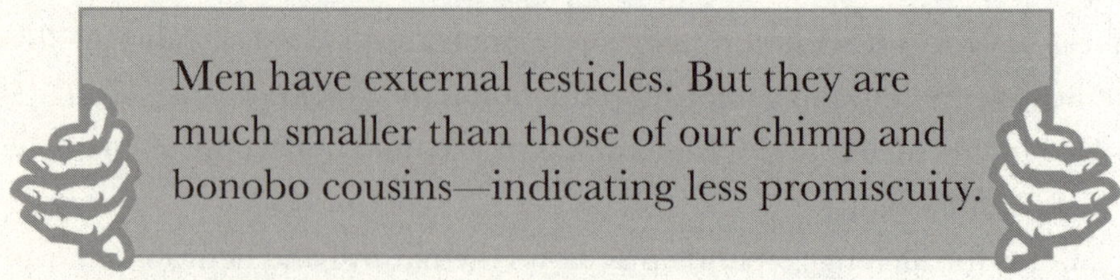

Ejaculation more than twice per day has been shown to dramatically lower sperm count in men. While there are occasional harems in human populations, these are mostly the result of status. They arise from the resources of a particular individual. But this is different than the species-level universal harems of gorillas.

Humans' basic tendency is towards serial monogamy.

Long periods of monogamy support the extended helplessness of human infants and children. Tireless and ongoing care is required by the mother, the father, and the surrounding tribe of relatives. A strong pair bond between the mother and father is necessary until the child can function on its own. We are not set up for lifelong monogamy, but we do invest in strong pair bonds for many years to raise children.

For his part, the father has to be highly certain that the baby is his before committing to its care. Most of the time, fathers get this right. There is historical evidence that the incidence of fathers raising a child other than their own is constant at approximately 1%. One adaptation that has helped is the tendency of the baby to look more like the father at birth. Fathers, and all their relatives, are more likely to accept the child if they share a similar appearance. By the age of two this effect disappears, and the child is equally likely to look like either parent.

Another way to guarantee paternity is to have sex with a virgin. The woman's intact hymen, although not foolproof, makes it highly likely that the first man to have sex with her is the father. Having an intact hymen makes a woman a more desirable mate in an environment of uncertain paternity.

When a man picks a sexual partner, a different kind of selection for long-term mates also takes place. Universal standards of female beauty include facial symmetry—indicating good genes. A childlike facial appearance with wider faces and larger eyes is also preferred. These infantilized features are a marker of youth and vitality. This is important for raising multiple children together.

Human breasts are another piece of the puzzle pointing to longer-term monogamous bonds. Women are the only female mammals with permanent breasts. Others have pronounced breasts only when they are feeding their young. Women get them before they are sexually mature, and keep them long after menopause. Most of the time they are filled with fat to keep their shape, and not the milk necessary for breastfeeding.

They are functionally superfluous. But women's breasts are a sexual signaling mechanism. Most primates approach their partners from behind. The human version of this would be the twin round swellings of the butt cheeks, spread, and making the vagina accessible for penetration.

But because people started to walk upright, the vagina also migrated towards the front of the body. The squatting presentation of the rear sexual view became much rarer. The surrogate twin mounds of the breasts migrated to the visible front of the body. A woman could be instantly recognized as sexually mature and available. This orientation also supported a stronger pair bond. Intercourse becomes a much more personal face-to-face affair.

However, the serial monogamy view is too simplistic.

Strong evidence also points to a significant degree of human promiscuity.

Let's clear something up—just because there is a tendency towards serial monogamy, it does not mean people do not like to have sex—a lot of it. Ninety percent of sex is recreational and not timed to the ovulatory phase. Women have concealed ovulation, and there is no evidence of an instinctual knowledge of the timing in humans. We even enthusiastically have sex when we know conception will not result—during pregnancy and after menopause. However, all this sex may not be with the same partner…

Here are some hints that promiscuity has always been fairly common:

- **Sperm blocking**—A tiny percentage of sperm race forward and may reach the egg in thirty minutes. Most sperm stay behind and form a mucous plug as a defensive position to keep the next man's sperm out. Sperm can survive inside the woman for 3-5 days.
- **More active sperm**—After being shown pictures of people having sex, men's sperm samples had a higher degree of motility (more active and mobile sperm). In the presence of potential competition, men build better swimmers.
- **Penis suctioning**—The human penis has a thick shaft and a wide mushroom-top of a head. This is very different from the tapering carrot penises of our bonobo cousins. On the backstroke of a thrust, the human penis can create a seal and suction out the sperm deposited by the previous man. There is even evidence that men thrust more deeply and quickly after incidents of possible infidelity.
- **Welcome-back sex**—When a man has been away from his partner for an extended time, there is an opportunity for her to have been with someone else in the interim. His sperm count during the following intercourse will be higher than normal. His libido is also higher—driving him to have sex as soon as possible as a way of insuring against possible outsider sex which may have occurred.
- **Male arousal at watching sex**—When watching a couple have sex, men get aroused. The visible prospect of a potential mating opportunity, even in a competitive environment, excites them.
- **Women's receptivity**—Unlike females of many species, women are sexually receptive all the time, not just when they are fertile. This extends even to times when they are menstruating. Women who are more available to their partners can keep their interest. This will minimize the likelihood that the men will wander off and have sex with others.

Hunting, gathering, and screwing

Let's take a peek at our past to better understand the conditions under which our pre-agrarian ancestors evolved their sexuality. This was our environment for millions of years. Despite the bewildering complexity of the modern world, our sexual evolution took place on the vast plains of Africa.

Small tribes of a few dozen people wandered around, only occasionally seeing other humans. There were no permanent settlements, so the groups were frequently on the move. The lifestyle had to be very portable. In addition to infants, only the most essential items could be carried, and they were shared among all tribe members as needed. Private property was not an important concept. Older adults who could not contribute or physically keep up were often left behind for the sake of group survival.

There was a lot more gathering than hunting. Foraging for food occupied most of the time. The active lifestyle, strong social connections, and a wide variety of foods resulted in a relatively long and healthy life. If, of course, you survived the pitfalls of birth and early childhood. Accidents, injuries, animal encounters, and infections were the leading causes of death for adults. There was no external wealth or possessions to measure against. Success consisted of strong friendships, alliances, and memorable social interactions.

Because of the small tribal size, status hierarchies run by domineering dictators were minimal. The cooperation of all group members was necessary for it to survive. Because of this, men and women were on a much more equal footing socially. Both were free to take on sexual partners at will. A woman could be intimate with several men and women over time. There was not a large choice of suitable partners within these smaller groups. It was important to maintain genetic diversity to avoid inbreeding. There is evidence that people find genetically diverse partners more attractive based solely on their smell.

Unknown paternity was a central feature of our evolution.

A good mother would continue to have sex while she was pregnant—possibly with multiple partners. This secured the paternal care and attention of many men in the raising of her children. Since a man could never be sure of exactly which children were his, each showed a wider and more equal concern for all youngsters. It was a small group with strong kinship, and the paternal lines often blurred. A man's orientation to others was an amorphous and unknown brother-cousin-father-uncle. In any case, they were probably his close relations.

Evolution does not care about you specifically. It does not operate at the level of the individual organism. People come and go, but our genes are remarkably stable and able to propagate themselves.

The most direct way to ensure the survival of your genes is to have children. The other way is to support the survival of close relatives who share some of your genes. Kinship ties were often close within each tribal group of people.

We devote effort to helping those most closely related to us. Here is where paternal uncertainty plays another key role. We are certain of the mother and the whole maternal line, since we can see who carries and gives birth to the child. If we look at the help we can expect from grandparents, a clear pattern emerges. Maternal grandmothers exhibit the biggest support. Paternal grandfathers offer the least. They are doubly uncertain—whether their son was theirs, and whether their grandchild was sired by their son. The maternal grandfather and paternal grandmother fall between the other two as would be expected.

High-risk sex

From the viewpoint of our genes, all sex is high risk. For life to continue, two things have to happen: an organism must mature and then reproduce itself. This is the most basic and powerful primal imperative.

All sexual species have some kind of preliminary qualifying event before mating.

They want to ensure only the fittest gets a chance at continuing their line. Some of these events are relatively tame—like the courtship song of a bird. Others involve direct competition among multiple suitors. Still others require the males to pay with their lives for a chance to mate and throw their genes into the next generation.

With so much at stake, powerful reptilian brain systems take over. The opportunity to mate is highly prized and all efforts are focused on it—overriding other survival goals.

When men are in a state of arousal, they become more impulsive, engage in high-risk behaviors, and focus on short-term payoffs.

The presence of attractive women undermines men's ability to use self-control or to delay gratification. This is true even when they simply see pictures of attractive mates. Men will also tune out anything in their environment that does not help them to achieve the mating-opportunity goal. When aroused, men are more likely to change attitudes about their willingness to engage in unprotected sex, or to get their partner drunk to make them sexually compliant.

Men think about sex a lot more than women. They are more likely to fantasize and imagine multiple sexual partners. They are also focused on the visual, with the emotional and tactile dimensions attenuated. Men also want to "get to it" more quickly and directly, to lock in their chance to reproduce.

Sexual asymmetry

Humans are a *sexually dimorphic* species. There are significant differences across physical, cognitive, emotional, and behavioral dimensions. Both sexes seek to impress each other, but in different ways, to be more attractive in the mating market. They will often go to extremes to do this—even at the risk of harm or damage to themselves.

The strategies that men and women use to attract mates are different. Men enhance their social status, while women enhance their appearance.

There are commonalities in what both sexes are looking for. Intelligence and kindness are high on the list. But other priorities are very different based on their expectations and needs from each other. The basic asymmetry arises out of their respective investments as potential parents.

In the extreme scenario, the man essentially has unlimited ability to produce sperm. So, his goal is to try and mate with as many women as possible. If there is a strong social group to support the mother, the man may be able to completely neglect the caretaking of his children. They would survive and even thrive due to the collective care of others.

Biologically, the woman is playing for much higher stakes. She has to carry the baby successfully to term, and avoid dying during childbirth. After this, she must provide for every need of the helpless infant, including carrying it and breastfeeding for many months or even years. To guard against this, parents are typically very watchful over their young daughters as they reach sexual maturity.

Men's signaling

The ability to protect and advance the long-term interests of their children is the quality women are looking for.

Women are attracted to high-status men, or those with the potential to become one.

Depending on the man's current social position, he will use the appropriate strategy to prove his desirability.

A high-status man will showcase his existing status.

If someone already has social dominance and significant resources, he will flaunt them.

- High-status clothes
- Luxury possessions and dwellings
- Social deference from others
- Lavish courtship gifts—an expensive engagement ring shows the suitor's tolerance for financial pain

A lower-status man will highlight his ability to achieve status in the future.

If you are not a dominant high-ranking male, you have to show the willingness to do whatever it takes to improve your social position. There have to be concrete demonstrations (usually in the woman's presence) for a potential mate to place her extremely high-stakes bet on you.

- Athleticism and willingness to take physical risks—extreme sports and painful initiation rituals
- Heroic jobs—soldier, fireman, policeman, lifeguard
- Financial risk-taking—gambling, day trading
- Physical dominance and aggression—willingness to fight, subjugate, or even kill others

Women are typically drawn to variations of this "bad boy" male earlier in life. But they will abandon them if the desired trajectory towards high status does not look likely to materialize.

Women's signaling

Women are in their own competitive war to attract the best mates. But their weapons are different from those of men.

Men are attracted to physical beauty in women—seen as a marker of youth and fertility.

Curvy or thin, we have already discussed the desire for swelling breasts and childbearing hips by men. The classic "hourglass figure" is seen as attractive not because of some shifting cultural norms, but as a deep-seated primordial scream inside of men—signaling the best mates to carry on their genes. Universally, the most attractive waist-to-hip ratio across all cultures falls within a very narrow .68 to .72 range. And before you start arguing this is simply some kind of objectifying visual aesthetic in our culture, understand that even congenitally blind men have the same preference and can detect it by touch. This is very primordial stuff.

The "hourglass figure" is the universally desired body shape, and women will modify their appearance to achieve it.

Women not endowed with these ideal proportions have disguised their weaknesses, or compensated for them in a variety of ways. The appearance of narrow hips can be widened by wearing ruffled dresses to create more volume. The butt can be tilted upward to create a more prominent and sexually accessible look by wearing high heels. High heels also make the legs look longer. This correlates with the preference of both sexes to be with partners whose legs are five percent longer than the average. Wide waists can be painfully cinched into tight corsets. A flatter bust can be surgically enhanced with implants.

The face also includes several markers of genetic fitness men consider beautiful.

Childlike symmetric features and evidence of arousal make women's faces more attractive to men.

Facial symmetry is an obvious one. If the genetic program contains few mistakes, the result will be more symmetric features. Wider and more prominent cheekbones and big childlike eyes are another indicator of youth. Youth enhances the likelihood that the woman will survive childbirth and have the vitality to care for a child. She could also potentially bear multiple children.

Signs of arousal, including engorged lips and dilated pupils, also make women more attractive to men, even if they are not consciously aware of it. This is one reason why many clubs and bars are dark places—the dim light ensures dilated pupils.

Women routinely practice a variety of techniques to create a younger and more desirable facial appearance:

- Hair coloring (to hide gray hair)
- Botox injections (to minimize wrinkles)
- Laser peels (to smooth and plump the skin)
- Collagen injections (to create fuller lips)
- Facelifts and eyelifts (to get rid of sagging and drooping features)

A variety of topical beatification procedures are also widely practiced:

- Bright lipstick (to draw attention to the mouth)
- Eye shadow and mascara (to create bigger-looking eyes)
- Foundation (to cover wrinkles and create younger-looking skin)

Dress and a variety of beautification rituals are used by women to increase their attractiveness.

The biology of love

Sexual arousal and love are not the same. They share some pleasurable feelings, but there are also important differences.

A variety of feelings and behaviors are activated by "falling in love":

- Intense pleasure
- Obsession

- Suppression of appetite
- Sexual desire
- Distortions in our judgment about the other person

We imagine their good traits to be extra good, and minimize their bad qualities. We like ourselves better in a romantic relationship. Everything takes on a wider emotional range—higher highs and lower lows.

A key brain region in this process it the *ventral tegmental area* (VTA). It should come as no surprise that it is rich in dopamine receptors and is part of the pleasure circuits in the brain. Falling in love has the same euphoric chemical effects as cocaine and heroin.

Our distorted view of our beloved also comes from the deactivation of the prefrontal cortex, which is involved in making judgments. Not surprisingly, this type of deactivation also happens in people with obsessive-compulsive disorder.

Romantic infatuation is a strong dopamine-based high which wears off for most people after nine to twenty-four months.

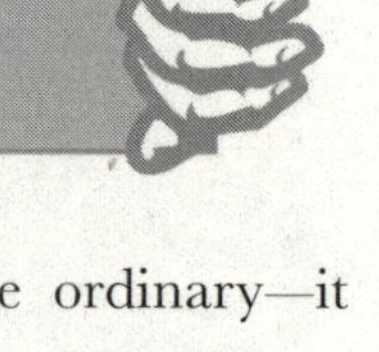

Afterward, the relationship mellows into something more ordinary—it becomes the new normal. A very small percentage of people can maintain the infatuation state for longer periods, but this is relatively rare.

Orgasms also produce intense dopamine-based payoffs, but are brief. During an orgasm the social reasoning and judgment centers of the brain are deactivated. Our body movements become uncontrollable. The "afterglow" of the experience releases oxytocin, and facilitates bonding and strong attachment. This is another example of nature repurposing the existing functionality of the brain (needed for the mother-child bond) for another purpose (couple bonding).

As with other events and substances which activate the pleasure circuits, sexual orgasms also create the potential for addiction. Sexual addiction runs the same course as opioid drugs. First, a tolerance develops, requiring more and more sex to achieve the same pleasure. Eventually, the pleasure turns into a compulsive need to get a frequent "hit," and is no longer some kind of mind-blowing cosmic union with another. Physical and psychological withdrawal symptoms can also result if the sex addict stops abruptly. The craving remains, and it is not uncommon for the person to return to compulsive sexual behavior again and again.

Chapter 16
LET ME TELL YOU A STORY

The functions of language

People conquered the world partly because of our unique language abilities. It is true that other species also have complex vocalizations, and relatively large vocabularies. However, they are mostly used for basic purposes like mating, displays of dominance, danger alerts, and soothing the young.

Human language is a powerful and flexible tool, and serves many functions:

- Substitutes for physical grooming to build personal relationships
- Serves as a low-cost way to practice social skills

- Communicates factual information
- Enforces causality and meaning on a chaotic reality
- Enables complex cooperation with total strangers
- Transmits ideas and values to strengthen cultural tribes

Our giant new brain capacity evolved to understand the dynamics of social groups. Among other mammals, harmony can be maintained primarily by grooming and physical caretaking rituals. In larger human groups, this breaks down. By some estimates, we would have to spend over forty percent of our waking hours just grooming each other to get the same social benefits.

Language allows us to verbally "groom" each other and requires much less time. An occasional "I love you" or "Great job on that report!" serves the same functional need without the large time investment. We have transferred the initial attachment from our mothers to a wider circle of people in our group. Their social praise and verbal acceptance serve to make us feel safe and cared for.

Storytelling and mindreading

Storytelling is a form of mindreading. We have already seen the ability of specific kinds of mirror neurons to mimic other people's actions. Stories go much further.

> When a speaker tells a story, the listener's mind shows the same pattern of activation—syncing up and following along.

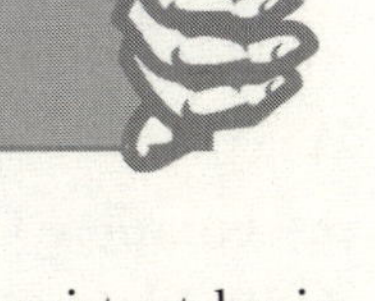

In speakers of the same language, storytelling syncs in a consistent brain pattern:

- Auditory centers (the sounds of speech)
- Early language centers (the understanding of words)
- Language centers (the syntax of sentences)
- Higher-order processing (extracting the meaning of the full story)

Speakers of different languages have the same meaning activations in their brains when they hear a translated version of the story. It's not the audible representation which is important, but rather the contents of the story.

However, on an important cautionary note, our specific belief systems will radically influence the interpretation of a story.

For example, imagine if you grew up in Spain. You heard the story about a famous matador who skillfully dispatched a ferocious charging bull with a deft stab of his sword. To you, the meaning of the story might be tied to the diligent preparation, skill, personal courage, and honor of the matador.

An animal-rights activist from another country would view the same story differently. They would think that it chronicled the wanton torture and eventual murder of a helpless animal. They might also despise the audience whose very presence allowed the brutal practice to continue. Same facts and storytelling—very different outcomes.

Without a common cultural background to interpret stories, the extracted meaning may radically diverge.

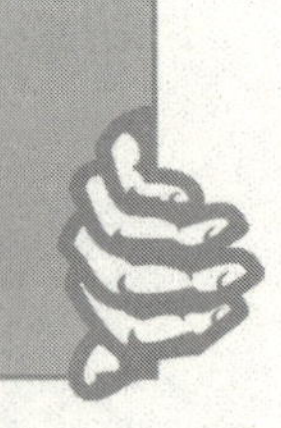

Whether the story is fiction or fact does not matter, nor the format of its presentation. Our distant ancestors were entranced by the stories told over the flickering flames of a small campfire. We can understand the written letter on the pages of a novel well enough to form a powerful vision of the characters and their experiences. Reading a story is akin to remembering or experiencing a vivid event.

We experience life as a three-dimensional movie unfolding linearly in time. Stories form enough of a framework for our minds to fill in the remaining blanks. We use narrative as a kind of second-hand reality.

We scream at unexpected dangers on the movie screen knowing that they are a part of a manufactured visual experience. We get engrossed in three-dimensional games and virtual reality worlds designed for us to explore.

Stories are a back door into our brains and profoundly change how people experience the world.

Consuming stories influences our beliefs, teaches us facts, alters our future behaviors, and changes our personalities. They insidiously shape our minds without our consent or knowledge. The more compelling the story, the more effect it has on us. People who are most absorbed in a particular story tend to mold their subsequent beliefs in a story-consistent direction.

You don't have to be a propaganda expert to understand that our deepest values can be changed by the stories we consume. They effortlessly bypass logical and conscious defenses, and shape our closely guarded core beliefs. Whether we actively choose them, passively allow them, or have them forced upon us, we cannot escape the powerful effects of stories.

Order out of chaos

We do not only get stories from the outside. Our brain also creates them. We are wired from birth to seek causality—the idea that events predictably follow from one another.

The brain is a meaning factory—we have a relentless need to explain the world and to create predictability.

Massive amounts of information are flowing into the brain all the time. We can't process it all, but we need to understand subtle patterns in the world. We look for causal explanations. This can get us in trouble if events truly are unconnected and random. Gamblers believe, incorrectly, in lucky streaks, and lose a lot of money. They are trying to impose order on inherently random and independent events like the successive rolls of dice.

The same is true of interpreting social events. Conspiracy theories come from our uncontrollable need to create compelling and meaningful narratives, especially if we feel powerless over our circumstances.

If we do not find meaningful patterns, our brain will impose its own—even if they are false.

Simulating social experiences

Hollywood is a powerful storytelling industry. Yet, interactive video games recently surpassed it in financial size. Potent simulations offer a more immersive type of storytelling. Through the ability to control the unfolding plot, games pack a powerful punch.

Simulation is key to human survival. As we have already seen, mirror neurons allow people to understand the actions and mental states of another, and practice what they are doing. Likewise, our nightmarish dreams give us a chance to confront threats and dangers in a safe environment. They prepare us better for responding to similar circumstances during our waking time.

Stories allow us to practice key skills needed in our social lives.

The vast majority of stories involve people, or animals with human characteristics. Many stories allow us to live out extreme emotional events without having to go through them ourselves. Powerful recurring themes include love, relationships, overcoming challenges, power, subjugation, and fear of death.

In stories we can experience strong feelings without paying a price.

All stories, despite the variety of superficial differences, share a basic structure. In a story, we want something and need to overcome obstacles to achieve it. The story reliably proceeds from complication, through crisis, and finally to resolution. In its own way, big or small, each story has a hero confronting some sort of trouble and struggling to overcome it.

Ecstatic love, despondent hopelessness, hate, and homicidal rage—all these and more are available to experiment with. You can be a remorseless killer, a pathological criminal, an upright person faced with a dreadful choice, or a hero willing to lay down your own life for the greater good.

Our hearts yearn for reunion with our distant beloved. We seethe with anger and disgust as we witness unbearable cruelty inflicted by the powerful upon the subjugated. Our pulse quickens and clammy sweat forms as we feel determination mixing with dreadful anxiety before going into battle against hopeless odds.

Yet in the end, we are still alive.

We poke at the last dying embers of the campfire, close the pages of a book, or walk out of the dark movie theater into the bright light of day, and we are unharmed. We have been deeply moved and maybe even profoundly changed. The story has been added to our storehouse of experience. We have had the opportunity to practice, without the risks of engaging in the actual behaviors.

Knowing a story is fictional doesn't stop the subconscious brain from processing it as real.

We seek out stories because they are inherently enjoyable. But their purpose is to offer us training opportunities to hone our social skills. Realistic rehearsal of any skill will improve performance. There are few things more important to human survival than rehearsing complex social interactions. Rewiring our brains through stories leads us to more skillful navigation of life's social problems.

Gossip, tribes, and civilizations

Language allows us to efficiently spread information about relationships within our group. We can determine who is friends with whom, who is a liar, and who someone is attracted to. This allows us to understand the ever-changing dynamics of the group, and keep track of alliances and dominance changes.

Popular gossip topics are universal:

- Substance use (drug abuse and drunken behavior)
- Sexual behavior (promiscuity, infidelity, secret homosexuality)

- Lapses in normal conduct (ethical transgressions and criminal behavior)
- Uncontrolled compulsions (such as gambling)

Most of the time we gossip about friends and close relations. But in modern mass-media societies we sometimes erroneously transfer this behavior onto celebrities. We obsessively gossip about them as if they were part of our ingroup. But we do not get the benefit of sharing actionable information or maintaining an accurate model of our place in the immediate group.

What many consider to be useless gossip is the universal glue that holds small tribes together.

In human tribes, the alpha does not win the position simply because of physical strength or aggression. Rather, their power depends on the amount of time and effort they expend maintaining social ties and strong coalitions. Language allows us to forge alliances, persuade, and keep track of favors owed and requested. Think of this as a personal level of knowledge.

We are much more adept than other mammals in forming larger and cohesive tribes through this kind of intimate communication. By some estimates, our close-group size is approximately 100-200 individuals. This seems to be the practical limit to the number of people with whom we can have direct, nuanced, and intimate contact.

However, none of this explains how people can cooperate on a massive scale. Yes, insects by the millions can cooperate, as can some birds and animals. But they are relatively homogenous, and guided by automatic instincts. They do not have specialized or complex individual tasks to accomplish within the larger task. By contrast, total strangers can step in and flexibly co-create behaviors which involve billions of people.

Language underpins this in the form of shared values and ideas.

Words can transmit an understanding of a shared imagined reality to total strangers.

Think of the concepts like religion, money, democracy, or justice. When you hear each of these words, it instantly throws up a gigantic shared edifice of related ideas and underlying values. The same cultural constructs exist in the minds of countless other people, and allows them to understand you.

Massive cooperation among people is only possible because of shared fictions and abstract concepts that we communicate to each other.

Just because something is a creative invention or a fiction, does not make it any less real. Nor is it a lie. As long as there is a shared community of people who adhere to certain ideas, the ideas can exert a strong force on their actions. Such social constructs can be powerfully held and believed. They can lead to significant individual and group sacrifices—including voluntary death.

Any large collective behavior is supported by common myths and stories that reinforce the values of the group.

A myth does not have to be about gods, or the creation of the world. It is any story that transmits and supports the values of the group through a common leap of imagination.

These myths can evolve and champion the emergence of new underlying values and behaviors. For example, just a few hundred years ago it was a widespread concept in many parts of the world that owning other people as slaves and treating them in the most horrific ways was acceptable. The myth of human equality and individual dignity spread. It gradually, and sometimes violently, triumphed over the myth of slave ownership.

In our time, the myth of unbridled capitalistic growth is colliding with the myth of planetary unsustainability. It is important to reemphasize that myths are not fictions, but rather shared stories which uphold the beliefs and behaviors among large groups of people. Our cooperation is almost entirely based on the stories that we choose to tell, and the prevailing myths around us. Stories bind us together and increase large group cohesion.

Chapter 17

THE DANCE BETWEEN YOUR BRAINS

Circling back to the very beginning of our story, it should by now be clear that there is no such thing as a purely "rational" mind." Much of the primal brain machinery works well for us. It is shared by many of our animal and insect relations precisely because it is so effective.

On the other hand, it is also clear that self-control, planning, insight, focus, creativity, concentration, and other "reasoning" aspects of the brain are a key part of our success. It is important to understand the strengths and weaknesses of both, as well as their interactions with each other.

For purposes of this chapter I will lump the evolutionarily earlier portions of the brain into one unit called the primal brain, unconscious, or autopilot.

> The unconscious mind operates automatically, constantly, and outside of our awareness.

The unconscious calls occasionally on the conscious mind—focusing attention on a specific task that needs to be dealt with. This only happens when our model of the world is inadequate—when our ability to predict is poor and the stakes are high.

> The conscious mind is largely on standby—only called upon to deal with important or novel problems that cannot be handled on autopilot.

Most of the time, the conscious mind does not find anything important to deal with, so it stays in a low-energy state and largely endorses the feelings and automatic decisions of the autopilot.

The conscious also monitors our behavior. It regulates our responses to others regardless of the underlying emotions which arise, and keeps us focused on goals that require sustained effort or concentration.

This energy-intensive portion of the conscious brain (largely contained in the oversized cerebral cortex of humans) is easily depleted and quickly loses its ability to function effectively.

The conscious mind can also call upon the subconscious and make use of its vast powers when needed. If the conscious needs to explore or search for something, it can also use the tireless machinery of the autopilot to accomplish part of the work.

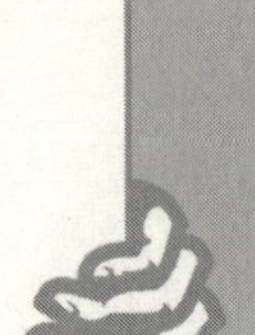

The effort to actively think about something is significant. The conscious brain often simply endorses the decisions of the unconscious instead.

Our emotional state is fed, along with objective information, to the conscious brain. We look only for information that supports our existing beliefs and attitudes. In other words, the conscious does not work in a vacuum, and does not concern itself with fair and complete investigation.

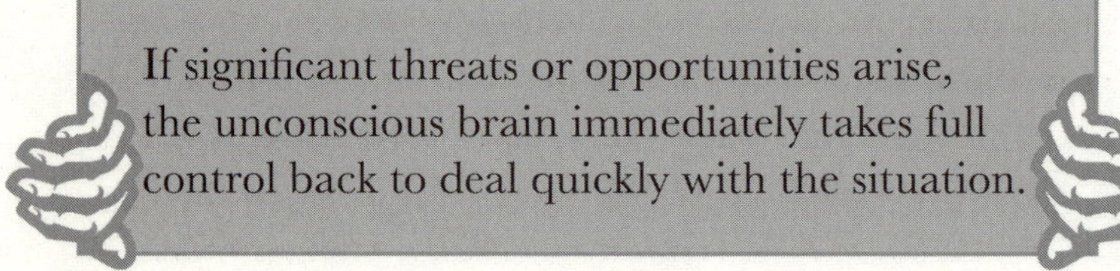

If situations are familiar, the unconscious deals with them appropriately. However, as you will see in the next section, there are some biases and tradeoffs which are required for the autopilot to operate.

Characteristics of the primal brain

The autopilot is always on, and processes massive amounts of information every instant of our lives. Most of this data never reaches our awareness. It remains as a background context which is taken in holistically. But it can influence our behaviors and decisions nevertheless. Even subtle or seemingly peripheral information influences our actions. The autopilot never gets tired and continues to work even when we are asleep—keeping basic systems like circulation, respiration, and digestion working.

> The purpose of the unconscious is to build and update a model of the world and use it to guide actions. To work quickly, it takes many shortcuts.

These shortcuts can be thought of as "good enough" mechanisms that work in most situations. However, in specific circumstances, these tendencies to oversimplify can lead to predictable biases and mistakes.

Let's look at some characteristics of the unconscious:

- Works quickly and without voluntary control
- Focuses on concrete examples and deals poorly with missing evidence
- Wants to create, and even invent, causality
- Responds skillfully to circumstances after repeated training
- Likes clear outcomes and suppresses ambiguity
- Ignores information that does not support existing beliefs
- Creates feeling-states and emotions based on past experience
- Overgeneralizes feeling-states beyond their proper origin and scope
- Responds more strongly to negative information than to positive
- Notices the unexpected and ignores the common or familiar
- Shows less sensitivity to increasing quantity
- Represents larger sets by prototypical examples
- Is more sensitive to relative changes than to absolute values
- Overweighs both very common and very rare events
- Substitutes easier decisions for complex ones

Characteristics of the conscious brain

The conscious or "effortful" brain operates on information which is brought to its attention by the autopilot.

To be examined by the conscious, information must first pass through two gates:

- It can't be dangerous—otherwise control reverts immediately to automatic responses
- It has to be unfamiliar—otherwise repetitive past exposure to similar situations will allow it to be handled routinely

Our conscious attention is very limited because the machinery of the cerebral cortex is so expensive to operate.

Once we become skilled at a task through extensive exposure and repetition, we have wired powerful superhighways of association into our brains. Different patterns of activation can be seen after such skill is acquired. Situations that would have once required conscious thought can be relegated to more efficient handling by the autopilot. This allows the brain to lower the demands on the conscious and to conserve energy in the future. What is appropriate to train for and commit to the autopilot depends on its value and the effort required.

You start your day with the ability to reason and make better decisions. You can also tune in to the complex social interactions with others and respond in nuanced ways.

Over the course of the day "executive function" and self-control get depleted and decline.

You are much more likely to make objectively poorer decisions, and are less able to regulate your emotions, later in the day. This problem is compounded by short or disturbed sleep. If you build up a massive "sleep debt," it must be fully paid off before the rational part of the brain can again work at peak capacity.

Conscious attention can only focus on one task at a time. There is no such thing as multi-tasking.

The more tasks you are trying to juggle, the more effort you are devoting to context-switching among them. This switching further depletes your limited reserves of attention. It forces you to make cursory surface-level decisions, which are often incorrect or suboptimal.

The focus on your current task can be very powerful, making you completely tune out other events that would normally call for your attention. It is possible to hijack attention by forcefully introducing another task. This will cause interference between the two. Such distraction tactics can be very powerful and significantly degrade performance.

Complex thought, working memory, and self-control all draw on the same limited reserves from the effortful conscious brain.

When you engage in difficult reasoning, try to memorize something, or regulate your social behavior, you are more quickly depleting the conscious brain. A little glucose can provide a quick boost, but is not a long-term solution. Only sleep can fundamentally replenish this reserve.

Once conscious reserves are depleted, more and more decisions are pushed down to the autopilot.

In our mentally tired state we don't realize that our subconscious responses may not be appropriate for the situation in front of us. We may display an exaggerated overconfidence in the effectiveness of our intuition. Under such circumstances we are more likely to yield to temptation and make rash, risky, selfish, or superficial decisions.

It is helpful to think of the unconscious as operating on "hot cognition," and the conscious operating as rational "cold cognition." As we discussed earlier, people (especially men) will make riskier and more impulsive decisions when mating opportunities are available. But hot cognition also applies to all significant threats and opportunities. The emotional processing in the amygdala has a greater influence on the prefrontal cortex than vice versa. Strong emotional arousal will dominate or even overrule conscious thinking.

Some people are wired to be less impulsive. Even as children, this can be a strong predictor of a happier life, higher incomes, and better social interactions. Less impulsive people do not experience emotions more weakly. They can simply regulate them better.

The prefrontal cortex can occasionally choose to suppress emotions and focus on specific problems or tasks at hand. It can think up novel solutions and recognize them as insights as soon as they are found. These insights can be recognized through its own efforts, or when others present them to us. After a conscious task is completed, the prefrontal cortex resets and prepares to handle the next one.

Working memory in the prefrontal cortex can manipulate and compute, but has very limited capacity. If flooded with too much raw data, it can no longer function effectively. Overload can have a paralyzing effect on choices and decision making.

Sometimes the prefrontal cortex overrules the primal brain inappropriately. This is commonly seen in sports. An athlete will start second-guessing and thinking consciously about their actions. Instead of drawing on the effortless skill of their trained autopilot, they try to outguess it instead. This is commonly called "choking," and is a result of the wrestling match between different areas of the brain.

At other times, overruling the primal brain can have very positive outcomes. The prefrontal cortex is also the home of the placebo effect. If we are told we are taking a powerful pain medication, the pain-sensing lower portions of the brain will be inhibited. This is true even if the "medicine" is just a sugar pill. Our conscious brain is telling the autopilot to experience less pain—a very powerful survival mechanism indeed.

This can also work in reverse. If something is thought of as being cheap, our conscious mind will associate it with being less effective and substandard as well. Our brain can force us to undermine its objective qualities.

Self-control is the last portion of the brain to mature.

Teenagers are notorious for their hotheaded behaviors. The strong emotions driving their actions are grounded in the primitive amygdala. The braking or inhibitory system resides in the *ventrolateral prefrontal cortex* (VLPFC). It does not fully mature until the early to mid-twenties.

The conscious mind decides where to direct attention. Sometimes it gives in to automatic impulses and responses. At other times it comes up with its own alternatives. Novel ideas and insights can only come from the conscious part of the brain.

The conscious will operate in a lazy-overseer manner to conserve energy. Automatic habits guide much of what we do to an astonishing degree.

But if something is deemed important enough, significant energy may be deployed in understanding it.

PART IV

HYPERSOCIAL

Chapter 18
HOW WE EVOLVED TO BE CULTURAL CREATURES

The common narrative of human dominance

Let me tell you a story…

Very smart primates climbed out of the protection of trees. They took tentative steps onto the teeming and dangerous plains of the savannah. By walking upright, they were able to use their hands to create and use powerful tools.

Weapons allowed them to defend against top predators and gather more food. Eventually these smart primates settled across vastly different environments. Their brains allowed them to adapt quickly to the changing circumstances.

They were also able to create sophisticated language and efficiently spread practical knowledge. They began to cooperate in larger groups, and to invent stories and shared fictional concepts like money and religion. This led to stable cultural tribes consisting of millions of individuals. Societies traded with each other—exchanging both goods and ideas. They were so successful that eventually the smart primates overran the whole planet!

It's a powerful story, but it is a work of fiction and misunderstanding.

It assumes that at some point, our evolution stopped. From there, our learned abilities got us to where we are. Growing knowledge allowed us to decouple from biology and step into the realm of history. Supposedly, our continued progress can only be understood through social, cultural, and technological developments.

But, to assume that evolution stopped and did not continue to play a massive role borders on willful blindness.

Where did we get this new knowledge to transmit to others?

How were we able to effectively spread it?

What accounts for the bizarre, and often unique, *biological* features of our species?

As we have already seen, our human ancestors were marginal players on the African stage. They were not smarter. They were physically weaker, slower, and had poorer senses.

Yet, they outcompeted every other species including our archaic human cousins. Unlike the brutish cavemen of popular imagination, Neanderthals were smarter as individuals. They had also tamed fire and could take full advantage of its benefits. They made art, fashioned tools, feasted on a variety of foods, and wore clothing.

But modern people won.

Let's take a look at some of the odd biological characteristics of our species:

- Babies are covered in massive amounts of fat
- We are helpless at birth and dependent on others for a very long time afterward

- Children experience rapid brain-building which continues into their mid-twenties
- We are remarkable imitators and faithful copiers of others' behaviors
- Our lifespans extend for decades beyond our reproductive years
- Our brains use three times the proportional energy of any other primate

Many of these characteristics developed recently and are *universally shared* among people.

This is an important point.

Consider the 200+ varieties of squirrels. They thrive from rainforests to semi-arid deserts. Some weigh 10 grams, others over six kilograms! Certain squirrels have webbed bat-like wings to glide from one tree to another. Others evolved 180-degree-rotating ankles to run down trunks headfirst. Still others hibernate to avoid the searing heat of the sun.

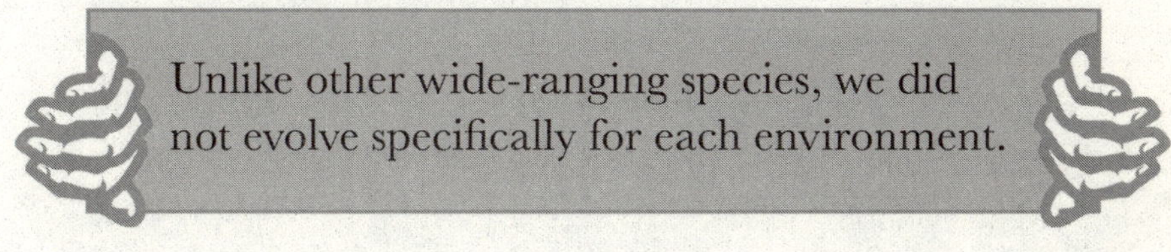

The pygmies of Cameroon average an adult male height of 150 cm. This is not radically different than the Dutch who measure in as the world's tallest at 183 cm. Yes, we have different coloring and features. But our minor physical adaptations pale in comparison to other animals occupying wide ecological ranges.

So how can we explain our dominance in every ecological niche on the planet?

Humans evolved brains that would benefit from cultural learning and transmission.

The success of people can be viewed as a single evolutionary bet on the ability to quickly spread knowledge. Tribal wisdom in our collective brains enhanced survival prospects in each particular environment.

The real story—cultural and genetic co-evolution

We are social learners—actively acquiring and trading information with each other. This has many advantages and countervailing severe drawbacks.

Learning from others allows us to efficiently copy "best practices" for our specific environment.

We can learn much more through our surrounding cultural package than we could have ever figured out in a single lifetime by ourselves.

That is our edge. The practices which are absorbed from surrounding people become increasingly more complex and powerful. Knowledge and effectiveness accumulate and over time create a positive feedback effect. Culture becomes cumulative.

But this advantage did not occur because of our individual brilliance. Rather, it arose from a sputtering and chaotic trial-and-error process across countless generations.

To be able to take full advantage of cultural learning we genetically evolved many characteristics over time.

- Bigger brains to store and communicate information
- A nuanced understanding of our social interactions
- The ability to automatically learn through imitation
- An extended opportunity to learn before becoming an adult
- Automatically understanding the best people to learn from
- Getting the cooperation of others willing to teach us
- A prestige payoff from teaching and transmitting knowledge
- A longer lifespan with an opportunity to teach others
- Knowing when to override personal experience and substitute learned culture

The end result of this process was the development of *self-domesticated primates* with the following attributes:

- Requiring a lot of interaction and engagement
- Pro-social and cooperative
- Assuming that we operate in a world of social norms and rules
- Having others monitor our compliance with the rules
- Enforcement of the social rules by the wider community

Blindly following a set of learned rules is at the heart of our cultural abilities.

It would simply be impossible to intentionally learn all aspects of the knowledge which we rely on.

Take cars as an example. To operate one, you need to understand the local rules of the road. You would master the operation of the steering wheel, gas pedal, brakes, transmission, and turn signals. You would need to know how to start the engine, operate the parking brake, and turn the engine off. This gives you the massive *practical benefits* of using a car.

Luckily, you do not have to understand any of the following:

- Finite-element modeling required to make the car's structure strong
- The chemistry and the properties of every fluid in the car
- Thermodynamics and the mechanical engineering of the engine
- Programming of the electronics, computers, and sensors
- The robots and factory processes required to manufacture and assemble the car

Even a lifetime of work as a specialized automotive engineer would not be enough to understand a tiny subset of the above. In our modern world we necessarily rely on an ever-growing array of increasingly narrow specialists.

We learn the useful aspects of our environment without understanding how or why they work.

Complex societies produce more knowledge, technologies, and specialized cultural packages to be learned by individual members. Other species can also organize on a large scale. Millions of ants routinely cooperate to create impressive works. But they are simple clones of each other and cannot learn. Only humans can accomplish massive cooperation among diverse individuals who are each programmed differently by early-life experience.

Big brains evolved for cooperative learning

We aren't born smart.

Human babies are not better at spatial relationships, quantities, or causality in the world than our great ape cousins. Our only edge is in social learning—actively seeking out and acquiring information from others.

Babies seem like useless blobs—drooling, pooping, and sleeping most of the time. But infants are actually very busy. They are devoting 85% of their energy to brain-building! The massive amount of body fat we are born with is used to insulate the electrical connections in our brains. This process is called *myelination*. If properly insulated, nerve connections become reliable and durable carriers of information.

Pre-insulation in the womb would seem like a powerful evolutionary advantage. It would allow more fully formed brains to function earlier in life. However, pre-insulation can only be done for automatic and unchanging brain activities.

To maximize cultural learning, our brain insulation is minimal when we are born, and stays flexible well into later life.

Chimp babies are born with about 15% of their cortex myelinated. People start with only a tenth of that! In the neocortex, which is disproportionately massive in humans, the difference is even starker. Chimps start with about a fifth already insulated, while humans are a completely blank slate, clocking in at zero. By the end of adolescence, chimps are basically done with major brain wiring. Humans are only two-thirds of the way to their final configuration, which is reached only in their mid-twenties.

Since humans are physically immature and inept for much longer periods, they are not learning as much by directly exploring the world. Our cues are primarily from watching other people. Babies and children intensely study and copy the behavior of adults and others around them.

People are frequent and automatic imitators, and expert copiers of others' behavior.

We even copy the purely stylistic elements, even if they do not seem to serve any apparent purpose.

The massive requirements of social-learning brains required borrowing energy and adaptations to the rest of the body.

- Weaker and smaller muscles
- Low-energy endurance running
- Smaller digestive systems
- A delayed growth spurt in adolescence

Let's look at these in turn.

Compared to our great ape cousins we are much weaker. A chimp scrambling on all four legs can easily outpace the fastest human sprinter. Pound for pound, they are about a third stronger. Don't let their smaller size fool you into picking a fight...

Among primates, we are the ultimate endurance running athletes. We may not be fast, but we can run for a long time, and outlast our intended hunting target with many specific genetic adaptations:

- Long legs with elastic tendons
- Energy-returning spring-like arches in our feet
- The most efficient sweating system of any species
- A specialized head cooling system
- Loss of most fur and body hair

- Reinforced lower body joints to withstand the repeated shocks of distance running
- Independent control of head orientation (where we need to look) and torso (the direction we are moving)

Our relative weakness and endurance abilities both stem from the fact that we have a higher percentage of *slow-twitch* muscle fibers. Breaking down a substance called ATP allows slow-twitch muscles to be much more efficient. They can operate for long periods sustainably. By contrast, *fast-twitch* muscles can result in short-term power, but are much less efficient. They build up lactic acid and tire quickly.

Our digestive system is really poor at almost every stage. We have weak jaws and fine teeth which are not good at grinding down food. Our colons cannot process fiber well. We cannot break down many powerful plant toxins that can kill us. We even call a part of our gut the "small intestine" since it is disproportionately tiny. The absorption of nutrients is the only normal part of our system—with an appropriate large intestine size. Yet, despite its many weaknesses, human digestion uses lower effort to extract energy from the food which we eat.

We remain in small childlike bodies for a very long time. It is only in adolescence that we grow to our adult size and mature sexually. This late maturation timing allows more energy to be used to wire up our flexible brains—making our bodies relatively cheap to maintain while we download the cultural package from our tribe and increase our chances of survival.

While each of the above seems like a logical response to the enormous energy needs of the bigger brain, they were not strictly genetic adaptations.

Our genetic adaptations co-evolved with culture.

Our digestive system could only shrink after we mastered fire and food-preparation techniques. Cooking effectively predigests food—making its energy easier to extract.

The act of running helped us to chase down specific animals, which were in many cases more powerful than us individually. But such hunting required projectile weapons, intricate group cooperation, and either carrying or knowing where to reliably find water. Water was needed to overcome the extreme cooling requirements of upright running.

The extended helplessness of children demanded huge investments in caretaking, feeding, and teaching from a large extended tribe of surrounding people. This required social organization, cooperation, communication, and a degree of apprenticing previously unseen among other animals.

There were several cultural evolutions, each with co-evolving biological adaptations.

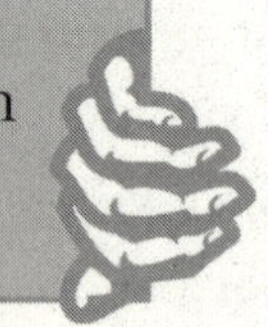

- Cooking and fire—a smaller digestive system
- Water finding and carrying—endurance running and hunting
- Projectile weapons—accurate throwing abilities and arm coordination
- Intricate tools—improved hand and finger dexterity
- Verbal communication—abstract concept understanding
- Language—ability to cooperate and not take advantage of each other

Evolution would not have invested in any of the biological adaptations if the culture had not offered compelling survival advantages in exchange. Culture-driven evolution can happen very quickly, as evidenced by the rapid emergence of blue eyes, lactose tolerance, and alcohol avoidance genes within the last 10,000 years. On the timescale of evolution, this is the blink of an eye.

How culture and genes caught fire

As cultural knowledge spread and multiplied, our genes moved in the direction of being able to take advantage of it. The race was on to be able to learn, store, act on, and transmit knowledge. Genetic evolution improved our brains and behaviors to be able to learn from others. Which in turn produced an even more powerful culture. And so it went…

But what was the spark which allowed it to happen?

Two important ingredients had to combine. First, the amount and quality of cultural learning had to be increased without the brain getting any bigger. Second, the cost of growing and programming bigger brains had to be offset or shared.

The key step was the one out of the trees.

Trees offered protection. Once on the ground, the world became a much more dangerous place for our ancestors. They began to congregate in compact larger groups to ward off predators. The social connections within the groups became stronger. The amount of time spent interacting with others skyrocketed. This increased both individual and group learning opportunities.

Extended time together allowed for the emergence of stronger pair bonds among people. It also spread the heavy burden of raising children among many relatives and other group members. As a result, children could stay helpless for a very long time. They acquired cultural knowledge from the whole surrounding group to powerfully program their larger brains.

This process was not linear. Doubtless there were setbacks. Key knowledge was probably lost countless times through cataclysm or forgetting. The end result was to produce practices that were smarter than any individual could develop by direct experience.

Chapter 19

THE BUILDING BLOCKS OF CULTURE

We stumbled along—making individual choices, having occasional insights, making discoveries through lucky mistakes, and mindlessly imitating over countless generations. Culture evolved, and from this process emerged the interconnected workings of several new abilities needed to efficiently learn from others. Take out any one of these pieces and the whole structure of cultural learning collapses.

To get better at using culture, we evolved several new mental abilities.

- Figuring out whom to learn from, and what to learn
- Learning by copying and modeling others
- Being motivated to teach others
- Knowing when to overrule our direct experience and instincts
- Consistently following social conventions and norms
- Noticing and sanctioning the cultural transgressions of others

Whom to learn from

From our first gasping breaths as newborn infants we are learning. But the questions which consume our whole lives are what we should learn, and from whom.

We try to copy more successful people. To find the best role models, we pay attention to a wide variety of cues.

We do this automatically, outside of conscious awareness, and independently of getting rewards for correct behavior.

Studies across many cultures and life stages point to a consistent set of learning preferences:

- **Cueing off of adult reactions**—Infants will explore new objects if the adult shows a positive emotion towards it, and back off if the adult shows concern.
- **Same sex**—Children and adults prefer to learn from and interact with same-sex role models. We inherently enjoy copying same-sex models, so we are more likely to do it. Children learn their sex roles because they copy same-sex models, not the other way around.
- **Same ethnicity**—Infants, young children, and adults all prefer to learn from co-ethnics.

- **Same dialect**—Kids prefer to learn from those speaking nonsense in their dialect instead of those speaking nonsense in a different language.
- **Relying on others' behavior when uncertain**—When we are faced with an unfamiliar situation, we are more likely to pay attention to the cues of those around us, instead of trusting our own experience.
- **Elders**—We pay attention to the wise older people. The most senior members of the community are often the most experienced. They survived a lifetime of risks and dangers successfully.
- **Acknowledged experts**—We key in on the practices of others and symbols of distinction to determine who is the recognized expert in an area of knowledge. Often, the person with the highest prestige is also a formal teacher. In this way, culture accelerates since the student not only learns the subject matter, but also the techniques for transmitting it to others.

In addition to the above, we also pay attention to others and look for information about whom *they* consider to be worthy models. In other words, we can culturally learn from whom to learn!

If our learning preferences seem self-reinforcing and closed to outsiders, it is because they are. One of the effects of such preferences is to quickly spread knowledge within our group. Another is to strengthen tribal ties and reinforce group cohesion against competing groups.

Teaching

Congratulations—you have successfully figured out from whom to learn valuable skills. Now all you have to do is put your ability to copy and imitate to good use, and you are all set!

Not so fast…

How do you gain the cooperation of your chosen mentor? Why should they allow you to spend any time around them? Why should they bother to teach you anything at all, much less let you suck a lifetime of hard-won knowledge out of their heads? Why shouldn't they actively hoard their knowledge and hide it from you?

To create a cultural chain, we must be incentivized not only to learn, but also to teach others. The mechanism for doing so is rooted in our need for prestige.

Prestige is a form of blessing others and paying your gifts forward.

Prestige internally motivates skilled individuals to share their knowledge with others. In exchange, they receive adoration, respect, and deference.

This motivation is so powerful that it is often a more important driver of behavior than wealth or other forms of overt power. The knowledge domains to which prestige can be attached are amazingly varied and flexible. We can become an expert in translating rare Tibetan books, making craft beer, or being financial advisors to professional athletes.

Prestige is very different from the dominance behaviors which we also share with other primates and mammals. Dominant individuals achieve their status through violence, threat of violence, or coercion. Others fear them. Lower-ranking individuals submit or offer appeasements to curry favor. Subordinates are reminded of their lower status via a variety of expansive body postures and behaviors by the dominant ones. The goal of dominance is to manipulate or bully others to achieve personal goals.

High-prestige individuals are rarely bullies, and are instead known for their generosity. Prestige is closely associated with success, skill, and deep knowledge about a chosen subject. People with prestige seek deference from those around them, and do not want to scare them off.

Because they have had a lifetime to acquire knowledge, older people are often important sources of information. They are a bridge to the future, and even when their bodies start to decline, they have valuable knowledge to transmit. Because of this, we generally respect older people for their wisdom. Most other animal species do not respect their elders.

This need to transmit cultural knowledge across generations has led to unique evolutionary pressure on people. Unlike any other primates, both men and women live two to three decades beyond their reproductive years. By shutting down the reproductive system, energy can be redeployed to transmitting culture.

At some point, our own mating opportunities become less important. We focus on strengthening the survival prospects of our children and grandchildren. During this time, our declining physical abilities are offset by our increased ability to transmit useful wisdom. This has its practical limits, of course. When cognitive abilities decline, the value of older people in transmitting culture also quickly fades along with their status and access to prestige.

There are countervailing pressures on the respect for older people. Their accumulated skills and wisdom are valuable as long as the world has not changed too much. This was the case for all of evolutionary history until very recently.

In our fast-changing world, older people's cultural knowledge becomes less useful, or even completely obsolete. Relevant cultural packages are modeled by increasingly younger people. They are closer to the edge of the freshest new knowledge. This inevitably strains the continuity and bonds between generations. It also leads to increasing ageism during a time when older people are living significantly longer and healthier lives.

Blind faith

Our cultural learning is often embodied in a series of procedural steps or practices which need to be carried out correctly. Which of those steps are vital versus purely ornamental is unclear. We can't easily discern their function, importance, or interconnectedness. In fact, in some circumstances it may be better if we don't understand their purpose, or how they work.

> We often have no understanding of why or how cultural adaptations work, or even that we are accomplishing anything beneficial by practicing them.

This lack of understanding of causal relationships impacts our psychology in profound ways. Natural selection has favored people who place their faith in cultural inheritance.

> The practices and beliefs of our tribe provide such strong advantages that we often override our personal experiences and intuitions.

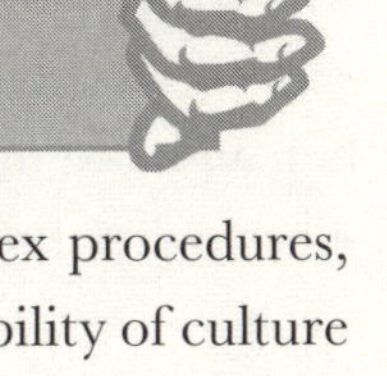

The end result is a strong instinct to faithfully copy complex procedures, practices, and beliefs. We evolved to take advantage of the ability of culture to construct complicated and subtle artifacts that give us a survival edge. This advantage is more powerful than anything we could have directly built in our lifetime.

Social rule followers

To take full advantage of culture, we have developed into a pro-social and very cooperative species. Maximizing the rapid and accurate spread of knowledge requires us to faithfully copy processes, rituals, and behaviors.

When dealing with the social world, people assume it is governed by rules—even if they do not yet know those rules.

Young kids pick up on social cues by inference. They assume these are based on clear rules and norms. Not only do children readily conform to these norms, but they get angry when the norms are violated, and seek to correct deviations by others.

We react with negative emotions towards deviants, even if we are bystanders and are not directly affected by their actions.

By the time we become adults, we have internalized the surrounding rules as internal behavior codes. This happens automatically. We regulate our behaviors to minimize the potential for personal social consequences. The emotion of shame guides us and allows us to become internally aware when we have violated norms. Often, displays of shame or public apologies are expected to correct our standing in the group. We are intensely aware of our reputation and guard it zealously throughout our lives.

Social sanctioning and punishment take on many escalating negative consequences depending on the importance of the violated norm:

- Gossiping
- Public criticism
- Damage to mating prospects or long-term intimate partnerships

- Reduction of economic opportunities and trading
- Confinement
- Excommunication from the group
- Death

We are wired to be cooperative and to prioritize group goals over individual advantage.

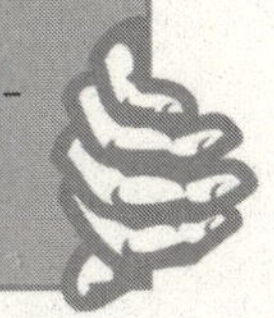

The opportunities for cheating are numerous. The more cooperative and trusting we are, the easier it is for others to take advantage, freeload, or manipulate us. Social norm monitoring and punishment by others is the evolutionary response to this.

The reward centers of the brain light up when we cooperate, give to charity, and punish norm violators appropriately. Through internal self-regulation and external consequences, we act in largely pro-social ways which benefit survival.

Violating norms requires more mental effort—using up scarce resources of conscious thought and executive self-control. As a result, most of the time we end up "doing the right thing" automatically, since it is simply easier.

Faithful adherence to cultural practices is vital for our collective survival. Everyone becomes a self-monitor, as well as an enforcer of others' compliance with accepted norms.

People faced with calamities, massive disruption, or uncertainty cling to their learned culture. It is an evolutionary response to help tribes to hold together to survive extreme situations.

> Under severe stress, people will fall back onto the social beliefs and rituals of their community, at the expense of personal experience or individual initiative.

If facts or direct knowledge contradict their cultural beliefs, people under duress will dig in even more. They will ignore objective reality. Faced with the choice of letting go of their learned belief or denying an incompatible new idea, they will choose the latter. They will behave better towards members of their group. They will also support their community interests against those of outsiders.

> The clash of cultural packages was a common experience in our evolutionary past. Intergroup competition is a defining part of our psychology.

The importance of group cohesion cannot be overstated. The larger the group, the more novel cultural ideas are generated. But for them to get maximum traction, they have to be able to spread completely and quickly through the group. To do this, the members of the group have to be harmonious and highly connected. We were bred for culture spread.

If you want to have the latest survival advantages, it is better to be social than to be smart. The perfect demonstration of this seems to be among our Neanderthal cousins. They were individually smarter and stronger than their modern human contemporaries. But they were pushed aside by the accelerating innovations of our cooperative communities. The collective hive-mind of Homo sapiens, along with our longer lifespans for transmitting culture, ensured this over time.

Chapter 20
THE SOCIAL NETWORK

Our brain is the ultimate social network.

Our success as a species relies on unprecedented cooperation among people. We cannot survive as individuals. Our core identity and behaviors are deeply influenced by those around us. We feel massive pressure to conform to group norms. Our deepest beliefs and attachments are shaped by common tribal allegiances, and we often protect them even at the risk of death.

Social thinking

Living in cooperative groups has both upsides and downsides. We get the benefits of shared efforts but we have to navigate the very complex world of intragroup dynamics.

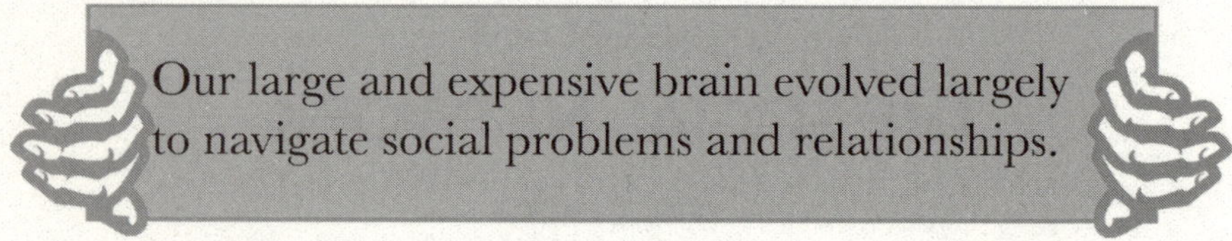

We can cooperate on monumental projects as unified teams, but huge effort is needed to create this unity.

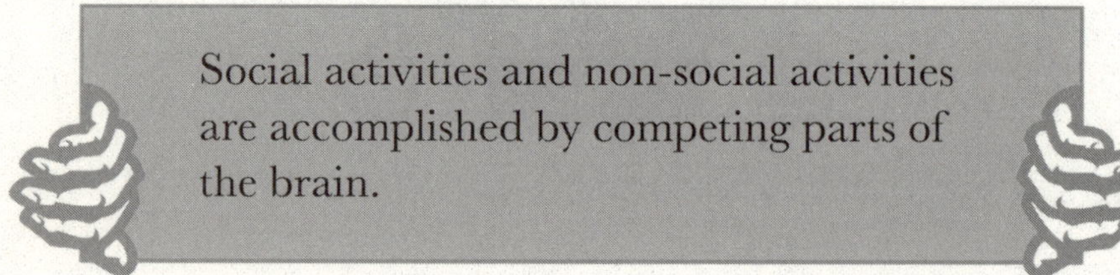

This tension plays out in many situations. If you are working on a non-social task to solve a problem, you largely shut down your social thinking. While you may be able to better focus on solving the problem, you may also alienate other people who might be able to help you with it. By focusing on direct problem solving, you may be losing the ability to fully consider the group's needs.

There is some evidence that people with various autism-spectrum disorders experience social information so keenly that it overwhelms them. Because of this, their brains shut down, scramble, or attenuate the flow of social information. This allows more energy to be devoted to non-social thinking. In some cases, this can lead to advanced abilities in art, music, design, engineering, and science.

The "nerds," engineers, and genius scientists of popular imagination may be the best solo contributors in their fields. They have extra mental capacity to deploy—freed from the burden of social thinking.

But their ability to cooperate, explain, and have others take up their ideas is more limited, and may require the assistance of socially oriented people. Since they spread new knowledge widely, the socially oriented people may be more impactful from the group's perspective.

If there is no immediate physical threat or computational task, the brain instantly and automatically reverts to thinking about social information.

Overlapping parts of the brain focus on solving visual tasks, motor tasks, and computational problems. As soon as these tasks are over, the brain quickly switches to other areas involving thinking about ourselves and our social relationships. All spare capacity and time are devoted to social cognition. That is our default mode whenever mental free time is available.

We use every opportunity to model and imagine our place in the social world.

Social thinking brain regions are actively working in babies within days of birth. Our brains are amazingly flexible, but we are prewired to take in new experiences through near-constant social processing, even before we become consciously aware of it.

No one is an island

We are the most social of all primates. Our giant neocortex evolved for understanding and updating relationships with people in our tribe.

We can have nuanced and connected relationships with approximately 100 to 200 other people.

In the nomadic hunter-gatherer societies from which we evolved, this was the appropriate community size. Bands of people had to be small, mobile, and very cohesive. Most tribal groups, and even modern organizations like operational military units, fall into this size range. We have personal knowledge of everyone in the group. We can manage our interactions through gossip, censure, and direct contact as necessary. No formal rules, laws, or complex codes of conduct are necessary in such situations.

It was only the advent of the agricultural revolution which ushered in a new age that allowed for larger societies. But underneath our modern civilization still beat the hearts of individuals who evolved to be in small hunter-gatherer bands.

Just because these bands were smaller, does not mean we did not need to cooperate to survive. In fact, we cannot be alone.

Social isolation has devastating effects on our mental health. Even before we literally go mad from complete isolation, our brains and behaviors change.

If people become socially isolated, they stop modeling and simulating the feelings of others.

What you end up with are impulsive, greedy, and self-serving behaviors—not a great combination. When forced to be unsocial, we start to behave in anti-social ways.

We have sophisticated brain systems for evaluating others' reactions towards us, and use them to construct our self-identity.

Reflected appraisal is the sum total of others' behaviors related to us. What is their tone of voice? What is their body posture? How closely are they sitting to us? What micro-expressions are passing across their face when they talk? What are they saying about us, and about others who are dear to us?

We use all of this information to understand who we are. Reflected appraisal is an ability that becomes very important during adolescence. When asked about themselves, teenagers access parts of their brain related to reflected appraisal. In other words, "who they are" is directly pulled from their model of other people's views of them! The impact of peers' views at this age is very powerful.

We have advanced systems for understanding others' views of us, and they actively shape our identity. In the West, the notion of an autonomous and independent individual is very popular, and we often think of ourselves as unique and important. We believe that the self is there to protect us against unwanted outside forces. In reality, this is not the case.

There is a hidden trapdoor in our minds that allows outside social influences to flood into our brains and mold our self-image.

Our conceptual sense of self is largely represented in the *medial prefrontal cortex*. This area also handles tasks related to cooperative activities—how to function most effectively as a group. Beliefs and cultural values involuntarily and unconsciously enter here from the outside world. The evolutionary goal is to make us into more harmonious cooperators.

Our "self" is essentially an overlay of various cultural influences that we are surrounded by. This can include our family, neighbors, coworkers, local groups, religion, and country. Rivers of cultural information flow into our minds and constantly reshape our conceptual identity and beliefs.

There is no solitary ego or personality to protect—we are wide open to continual cultural shaping and cannot stop it.

The tug of war will never end. Our individual needs and self-expression are at war with the need to conform to our group norms and to fit in.

The need for belonging and validation

Attachment is a serious business for all mammals. But it is crucial for people, since we have such long and physically helpless extended childhoods.

The dACC (*dorsal anterior cingulate cortex*) keeps track of whether our needs are being met. If they are not, it raises an immediate alarm. One of the conditions which sets off the dACC is social separation.

We experience social separation as acutely painful. This evolved to keep high-need infants and their parents close together.

But this mechanism does not simply go away as we mature. We continue to require massive amounts of healthy social attachment and validation. Many mental health issues stem from formative experiences in which a child did not get appropriate support from caregivers. This damage is often difficult or impossible to undo, since it wires the brain differently at a physical and chemical level.

Our need to belong and feel loved is central to our well-being.

Those who have been bullied as children are several times more likely to commit suicide by their adult years.

We even get influenced by total strangers with whom we don't want to interact. If they tell us they like us, the brain's reward system is activated. We have an unquenchable thirst for appreciation and validation. When appreciation is reciprocated, it brings us closer together. Unlimited amounts of appreciation and flattery can be directed at others, and reflected back from them—keeping us socially bonded.

Synchronous group activities bond people together.

Have you ever watched a group of people performing tai chi? There is an unmistakable unity and connection among them. You can see the same in a yoga class, choir practice, religious ritual or group prayer, or watching spectators doing the "the wave" at a large sporting event.

The trick is in the doing. Our mirror neurons kick in and model the movements and the mental states of the other people. You don't have to like or know the other participants in the group, or even enjoy the underlying activity. The synchronous actions will still result in bonding, which will strengthen social attachments. The personal feeling is one of well-being and connection. The evolutionary result is an increased chance of group survival.

Peer pressure and conforming

Many of us like to think of ourselves as autonomous and independent in most circumstances. In reality, this is not the case.

Most people look to others to decide how they should behave.

We are likely to fall back on the cultural values and behavior of others around us. This is especially true in times of stress and uncertainty.

External accountability creates additional pressure on top of our internal feelings. We are aware that we will more likely face consequences for non-compliance if we are judged publicly.

We are more likely to conform when we know our actions are being witnessed by others.

The strongest social currents to swim against are the us-against-the-world variety.

If the group's behavior is unanimous, we find it even harder to resist its example.

Confidence is also a major factor.

Consistency and unwavering belief on the part of a few key individuals can move a group's behavior.

Sometimes these initial starting conditions can unintentionally harden into "traditions." A few confident individuals sway the group. The behavior then becomes widely practiced—perhaps even unanimous.

Afterward, it becomes very hard to dislodge this established precedent. If something becomes popular, equally good or even superior alternatives have to struggle for acceptance. This is solely because they did not reach the critical mass of social consensus first. Since people look for popularity as a gauge of "social proof," it is hard to overcome the initial lead created by the popular practices or ideas. Small perturbations, or random luck at formative stages, can produce huge variations in the adoption of beliefs and behaviors.

Ingroups and outgroups

There is an inherent tension between the needs of the individual and their group. But equally important is intergroup competition.

Us versus them—our evolution is repeatedly marked by the survival of the most effective groups against competing ones.

As discussed earlier, oxytocin is not simply the "cuddle" chemical of popular imagination. Yes, it creates a strong bond between parents and children, as well as other members of the ingroup. But it also actively fosters hostility towards members of outgroups.

People strive for belonging in groups. They can easily self-sort into competing "tribes" based on the most trivial differences.

This group loyalty can develop very quickly, and even form around meaningless beliefs and actions. We quickly become cheering fans for our sports team, and mock people who are on the other side of our affiliation. We will actively build walls and boundaries to protect our newfound beliefs. The more visible and external these differences are, the easier it is for us to feel superior to people in other groups.

Religious faith and belonging has additional evolutionary support within the brain. The *insula* is a brain region that seems to be connected to our experience of a unitary divinity. The *candidate nucleus* produces sensations of joy, love, and self-awareness. These combine with group belonging to form a powerful basis for religions as a form of social groups. Belonging to a religion can produce strongly held beliefs and profoundly impact our behaviors.

Having a clear enemy allows us to both demonstrate our faith and unite strongly against an outside threat.

Many escalating strategies are used to "win" in the spread of ideas, behaviors, and cultural packages among groups:

- **Evangelism**—Actively spread ideas through outreach to demonstrate the advantages of belonging to your group.
- **Vilification**—Actively focus on falsehoods, or emphasize the worst qualities of other groups.
- **Breeding**—Have more children who are raised within your belief system. This will outcompete other groups over time through population pressures.
- **Forced conversion**—Coerce people into complying with your codes of behavior, and suppress alternative expressions. This is often done by forcibly taking younger children out of their original group to indoctrinate them.
- **Excommunication**—Banish non-conformists to the edges of the group or exile them.
- **Subjugation**—Deny key rights or freedoms to members of outgroups. In extreme circumstances the result is slavery. This includes sexual violence and sanctioned rape.
- **Death**—Kill enemies in open warfare or low-grade conflicts.

Groups' behaviors against outsiders are often harsh and brutal.

Our need to band together to compete against other cultural groups has remained a deadly serious and ongoing evolutionary business.

Chapter 21
OWNERSHIP, FAIRNESS, AND FAVORS

Ownership and possession

Imagine you are on the African savannah 100,000 years ago—with the rest of your small tribe and trying to survive. What would you carry with you? Whatever you chose had better enhance your survival prospects. Unfortunately, you have to carry the useless, blubbering, and farting baby, since it is not able to survive on its own yet. What else? Would you carry food, water, a weapon?

Perhaps you found a good-sized rock with a razor-sharp edge which would make a great weapon or tool for skinning animals. Should you pick it up and carry it? It is not an easy decision. On the one hand, it is a good fit in your hand, and would make a wonderful tool. On the other hand, it is pretty heavy, and you are committing to carrying it with you everywhere you go for the foreseeable future. You are constantly on the move—walking an average of about ten kilometers per day, like the rest of your contemporaries. The energy expenditure required to carry the rock is significant.

Possessions came about as a result of significant effort, time, and commitment. If we own something, we feel that it is vital to our survival and overvalue it.

It gets even trickier to make the carry-the-rock decision. Perhaps there is a shale field with plenty of similar sharp rocks just out of sight ahead of you. Or you might be walking into a flat terrain with only sand and clay, and such a rock will not be available ever again. We have a deep fear of missing out on opportunities.

If something is uncommon or scarce, it assumes an extra value in our brains.

When we own something, we value it more than other people do. Our focus shifts to zealously guarding what we already have, and not acquiring something new. As we have already discussed, fear of loss is a more powerful motivator than gain. It is approximately twice as powerful depending on the circumstances.

Overvaluing possessions is rooted in our need to prepare for an uncertain future.

In the modern world, these evolutionary impulses often lead us astray. We no longer have issues carrying or transporting items. The trunk of the car or the flatbed of the pickup truck are pretty large. Nor do we worry about acquiring items—efficient marketplaces for any kind of object can be found. And we do not have problems storing our objects. Overstuffed closets, pantries, workshops, garages, and huge storage unit warehouses attest to this. We hoard and "collect" a bewildering number and array of items.

Ownership does not have to be literal. Other factors can influence our psychological sense of possessing something.

Physical touch and the handling of an item makes you more attached to it. Trying on clothes or test-driving a new car simulates perceived ownership and generates positive emotions. Anticipation stimulates the imagination and makes you feel like you already own an item as you simulate its use. Positive discussion and active visualization of such a future can also influence the speed and degree of attachment.

Fairness or revolt

We are evolved to be highly cooperative. However, there is always a tension between meeting our individual needs and those of the group. We could always choose to act in a greedy and self-serving way. But we might lose the immediate and long-term benefits of cooperation with others.

We expect to be treated fairly. If we feel that we are not, we will violently refuse—even against our own best interests.

If looked at from the standpoint of individual benefit, this seems like a maladapted response. After all, "half a loaf is better than none." And by the same logic, even one one-hundredth of a loaf leaves us individually better off—so we should accept it rather than nothing.

Yet, there is a lot of evolutionary pressure to make our species cooperative. Our primate cousins are also wired to reject unfairness. We would rather get nothing, or even negative consequences, than accept an unfair result. The emotional impact of the unfairness outweighs any tangible benefits gained.

An intolerance for unfairness drives us to correct the situation.

Unfairness is like an itch we have to scratch. When we witness or experience it, we often have a disproportionate response which continues to nag at us. The *anterior insula*, along with other brain areas, is involved in processing these feelings. The indignation will continue until we resolve the situation.

The *superior temporal sulcus* part of the brain helps us imagine and sympathize with the emotions of other people. We feel another's happiness resulting from our generosity—even though it required our sacrifice. Mirror neurons allow us to get inside of other people's heads by simulating their emotions. We have a strong need to create these empathic reactions. We even generalize them to stuffed animal toys and computer programs.

Altruism feels good—in some cases, giving something away actually makes us feel better than keeping it.

There is a part of our brain called the *ventral striatum* which is highly sensitive to the overall rewards to the group—and not to ours as an individual. This counterbalances our need to maximize personal value in every exchange with others.

As long as the result falls somewhere within the "fair" range, we will prioritize overall group outcomes through cooperation.

It feels good to help others that we care about. When we think about cooperation, we often focus on the benefits we receive from the support of others. But there is another benefit.

Serving and supporting others contributes to our feelings of well-being.

In addition to being self-serving, we experience the welfare of others as an important internal goal.

Social and transactional spheres

Under what circumstances do the social considerations apply? When are we likely to be more selfish and individually focused?

We operate in two separate and incompatible spheres—social and transactional exchanges. Each one is governed by different norms.

The social sphere involves ongoing, perhaps lifelong, interactions with a relatively small number of our ingroup tribal members. The transactional sphere predominates when we are dealing with strangers or people with whom we do not expect regular contact. In the social sphere, we do not require a favor or obligation to be immediately discharged. In the transactional sphere we do.

Imagine two similar situations: You are a highly paid expert in a particular area of knowledge. A friend comes to you and needs your help. In the first situation, they simply ask for your help. In the second, they offer to pay you half of your regular rate. The outcomes are predictable. If they simply asked for your help, you would likely comply and feel great because you could share your vast expertise. If they asked for a reduced rate, you would most likely feel resentful and undervalued, and would be less likely to help them at all.

Imagine two more situations: A friend brings you a small gift, and you thank them. In the first situation they mention they got that gift because they thought specifically of you, and knew you would like it. In the second situation, they mention that it was not a big deal because it only cost a small amount of money. Again, the outcomes are predictable. In the first situation, you would be grateful. In the second, you would feel slighted or resentful. Social relationships damaged in this way are very hard to repair.

Mention of financial considerations moves interactions from the social to the transactional realm. They remain there for a long time afterward.

Once money is mentioned, people become more selfish and self-reliant. They want to spend more time alone or working on solo activities.

Reciprocity and obligation

Many animals trade and share food to help each other. Of course, the dominant individuals get to eat first, but after they are stuffed, they may offer the scraps to others as a sign of their magnanimity.

When someone does something for us, we feel obligated to return the favor.

But this does not explain human reciprocal altruism. It consistently extends over time, and is not simply concluded during the moment of exchange.

Unlike other animals, we keep track of the obligations we incur. We are uncomfortable and even a bit anxious until we discharge or repay the debt. This is a universal human behavior norm and likely grew out of our need to cooperate when famine or hunger conditions prevailed.

The return of obligations can take a wide variety of forms.

These include food, teaching of skills, trade, gift-giving, alliances, defense, caregiving, or even unspecified future favors. Our ancient ancestors created webs of indebtedness and complex networks of obligations which were expected to be honored.

The power of future obligation allowed people to give away resources without actually losing them. They could reliably get cooperation through generous gestures.

Reciprocity and hospitality are easier when you are taking care of close relations. However, for people to extend the same cooperative options to non-kin, certain evolutionary conditions had to be in place:

- We have to be intrinsically motivated to give and enjoy the act of giving
- There have to be repeated interactions—including a future opportunity to return the obligation
- We have to recognize particular people and remember the obligations we owe to each
- The need to return the favor should not fade too quickly over time—especially for larger or more memorable obligations
- Our reputation for integrity is important social capital—so we can be expected to honor our commitments
- An initial gift has to reliably trigger an obligation of equal or greater value

The last point is important.

Gifts trigger indebtedness, even when they are not invited.

If the person offering an initial gift was consistently shut down and no value flowed back to them, the whole system would break down. From an evolutionary perspective, even uninvited obligations have to compel reciprocity. Although it doesn't always feel joyous or completely voluntary, it is very hard not to return an uninvited favor. In a very real way, we cannot choose whom we become indebted to. The power rests in the hands of those initiating the exchange.

If we did get a consistent payoff, but it was smaller than the value of our initial gift, reliable cooperation could not develop. Evolution has biased exchanges in the direction of the initial gift giver for the group to benefit from being highly cooperative.

A small initial favor can often result in a substantially larger obligation in return.

Since there is a biasing towards giving back more value, this tendency can often be exploited. Samples are a perfect example. If someone tries a product or service and has gotten benefit from it, there is a strong resulting urge to buy it. The "free" sample puts chains of obligation on us.

This approach is also highly effective as an escalation technique and is tied to our sense of personal integrity.

People who comply with a small initial favor are more likely to grant a much bigger follow-up request.

Chapter 22
CONFORMITY AND INTEGRITY

The inner lives of others

In the West there is a widely held cultural belief that individuals are the basic unit of society. Our particular lives matter, and how we uniquely express ourselves is the key to our happiness. To conform is seen as a weakness of character or a lack of willpower. In reality, this very notion of the independent person was an idea snuck into our heads by our surrounding cultural tribe.

By contrast, in the East, societies are organized around more evolutionarily natural group norms. People are expected to harmonize with each other to have the best chance of creating effective community living. The brain region linked to our conceptual sense of self is swayed by social influences, and there is nothing we can do to prevent this.

> The social signals we get from surrounding people profoundly shape our behavior, even when we are unaware of them.

We are highly attuned to people's voices, gestures, and facial expressions. Faces, in particular, offer a wide array of information. Universal innate facial expressions provide us with information about people from the outside. The *fusiform face area* (FFA) allows us to take disconnected features and recognize a specific face or emotional expression. This is combined with information about the person's identity and our history with them. Through the use of mirror neurons, we can instantly create empathic states simulating their feelings, and respond appropriately. This gives us vital clues about how to act.

The ability to accurately recognize people's emotional relationship to us critically depends on a proper night's sleep. If we shortchange the sandman, we will wake up the next morning with a more paranoid orientation. Even neutral expressions will evoke feelings of fear or potential threat.

Group power

As we discussed previously, we are highly cultural creatures. Wielding the accumulated knowledge of our tribe gives us a survival advantage. Culture is much more powerful than anything we could recreate by direct experience in our lifetime. To transmit culture, we have to assume there are social rules and norms, and to conform to them.

> We determine the correct behavior by modeling others. Individuals will often change their beliefs, opinions, and actions to conform to the group around them.

We look primarily for two types of cues to determine when to act on such "social proof."

> Popularity and the behavior of a group of people is a reliable guide to making choices.

Our need to conform is strongly tied to the number of people around us who are carrying out the behavior in question.

As noted earlier, we pay more attention to teachers and role models who are our same gender, who speak the same language, and who are co-ethnics.

> We are more likely to be influenced by people who are the most like us.

This effect is most powerful when we don't know what the correct social behaviors are for a particular situation. Under these circumstances we seek safety and want to avoid unexpected negative consequences. So, we pay extra attention to how others around us are behaving.

When we are unsure of ourselves or our surroundings, we are more likely to be influenced by others.

Social norms can work in both directions. If we somehow find our performance to be substandard compared to the group, we will redouble our efforts. However, if we find that we are ahead of the group norm, we will slack off to fit in better.

Integrity and consistency

As we discussed earlier, the critical mechanism of reciprocity relies on future obligations. We have to remember and discharge the debts we incurred from others. Likewise, we have to be able to count on their willingness to honor their word.

We have to be able to rely on the integrity of others—their willingness to act consistently and honorably.

The very word "consistency" conjures up related qualities of dependability, discipline, and predictability. By contrast, an inconsistent person can be characterized as flaky, random, unstable, fickle, or unreliable—hardly a flattering inventory.

Inconsistency is not just damaging to the reputation of the individual. It also brings massive social pressure to bear.

Our need to conform to group norms demands that we carry ourselves consistently.

If someone is not in accord with the behaviors and beliefs of the group, they are, by definition, a poor team member. Severe social sanctions will often fall on such people. They will either be forced to conform or removed from the group.

Once we formulate a position, there is strong pressure for us to stay consistent with it.

Even subtle small leanings in our initial thinking can quickly harden into firm beliefs and behaviors.

To create consistency, we have to commit. The strongest commitments are freely chosen, public, and involve sacrifice.

If these conditions are present, we will feel a dual pressure. Our internal self-image will want to remain in integrity with our actions. The external perceptions of others will also force us to comply. After such commitments are formed, they do not need much maintenance. We operate on autopilot until we are forced to change the belief again in the future.

The seeds of voluntary action

Mighty oak trees grow from single seeds.

In much the same way, powerful commitments originate in small voluntary actions.

Getting a small voluntary commitment will make it much easier to get larger ones later.

As we have seen above, it is very hard to change someone's ingrained beliefs. The best way to proceed is via a sneak attack—start small and build.

If someone makes a voluntary commitment, their self-image is instantly shaped by the action.

This starts a snowball effect, and more significant actions consistent with the first become possible. Such progressively escalating commitments create a momentum of compliance which can result in massive changes.

As we get older, our need to remain consistent with our commitments seems to increase. It is unclear whether this is due to decreased plasticity of the brain, or is the result of mental energy conservation.

Making a public stand

We are constantly being watched and judged by others. Peer pressure, conformance to social norms, and sanctions for failure to comply make up our daily world.

> The more public our commitments are, the more strongly we will stick to them.

Raising a hand, a verbal utterance, writing something down, or signing a document will all increase our likelihood of acting consistently with our declarations.

> Knowing that our actions will be witnessed by others is a very powerful force.

Self-sacrifice

Are you in, or out?

Are you in it for yourself, or looking out for the well-being of your tribe?

Answers to questions like this had life-or-death consequences throughout our evolutionary history.

An effective way to gauge someone's commitment was to put them through a test. If they were willing to sacrifice their self-interests for those of the group, they were judged to be reliable, and were accepted.

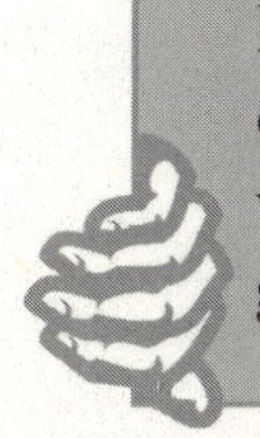

> If someone is willing to go through a great deal of pain or trouble to get something, they will value it more highly than a person who gets the same through little effort.

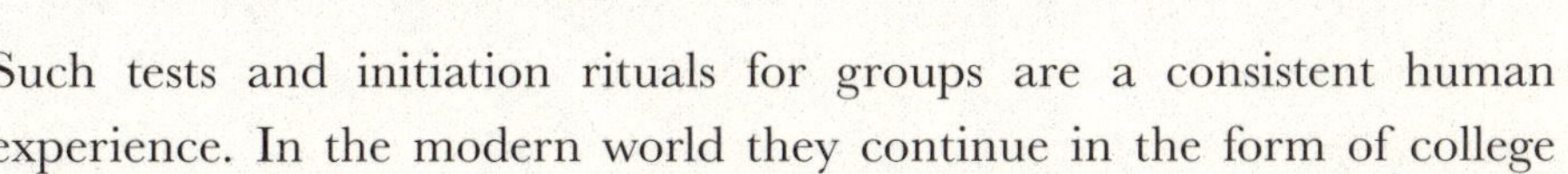

Such tests and initiation rituals for groups are a consistent human experience. In the modern world they continue in the form of college fraternity hazings, gang jump-ins, and various military boot camps. They persist because they are designed to approach the limits of physical exertion, psychological strain, and social embarrassment.

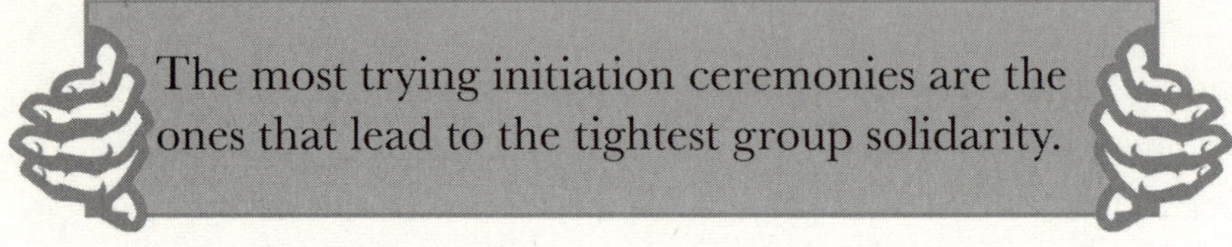

Sacrifice heightens the new member's commitment to the group and creates a sense of accomplishment and pride. The difficultly of obtaining acceptance makes group affiliation attractive to potential future members.

PART V

WHAT'S NEXT?

Chapter 23

HOW TO BE MORE PRIMAL

Thank you for letting me be your guide for our primal brain discovery adventure!

I hope you have learned something new, and shifted your perspective about your fellow humans. Applying the knowledge in this book to particular domains would require many additional volumes.

However, I would like to leave you with some quick thoughts about how to be more personally effective and fulfilled. These are meant to be directions for you to explore, now that you understand why they are fundamental to your humanity.

Get proper sleep

Want to be a paranoid and aggressive jerk? Want to be dull, unable to learn, and lack original or creative thoughts? Want to be more likely to get injured, suffer from a wide range of diseases, perform poorly at physical skills, and die prematurely?

You can have this and much more, simply by not getting regular and adequate sleep!

Sleep is foundational to all animal life on earth. Yet as "modern" humans we regularly shortchange ourselves. Our natural light-and-dark-based rhythms are overridden by artificial lights. We mistakenly think we are being more "productive" by staying up late into the night.

Unfortunately, this "sleep deficit" can never be fully repaid. The damage we do to our brains and bodies is cumulative, and affects many aspects of our lives.

Our hypersocial natures depend critically on the ability to read and understand other people's nuanced emotions. Without the benefits of proper sleep, we cannot function as individual people, or build an effective and healthy society.

It's dark outside. Put down your phone. Don't binge-watch another episode of your favorite show. Turn off the lights.

Just go to sleep.

Be in your body

The brain is often thought of as the superior puppet master, and the body merely as its obedient servant.

This artificial separation does not exist.

Evolution shaped you at the genetic level. While the brain is an important body component, it is merely one of many. Without circulation, respiration, and digestion you would not be here.

Although the focus of this book has been on the brain, the central nervous system extends into numerous body systems. It gives orders and collects feedback in an ongoing dialogue. Voluntary muscle control nerves extend to the very tips of your limbs and allow you to move through the world. Your brain is everywhere, and it is part of a unified organism.

The body truly is a temple, and its healthy maintenance is required for peak brain performance. As I mentioned above, sleep is foundational for both brain and body maintenance. On top of it, regular exercise and a healthy diet are also key.

Almost every Olympic-level athlete incorporates weight training into their regimen. Our muscles contain the nerve cells that control them. The only way to reliably enhance and repair these neural connections is to tear up the muscle tissue in which they are embedded. By straining and rebuilding the muscles, your nervous system and brain are improved. You cannot get this benefit by participating in cardiovascular exercise alone.

If you exercise, you should consider doing as much of it outside as possible. We evolved to feel safe and energized by moving through the natural world. Our modern lifestyles require us to spend most of our time in structures and vehicles. These are specifically designed to keep the natural world out. There is growing scientific evidence that decreased time outdoors negatively impacts our mental and physical well-being.

Get outside, and get moving.

Regularly access your intuition and emotions

Except for survival-level crises, all of your decisions rely on your ability to tune into feeling states. The rational parts of the mind are largely asleep, and the deep pre-verbal wisdom of your unconscious largely runs the show. Emotions reliably dictate your affinities or aversions, based on past experiences and memories.

Unfortunately, most of the time we are unaware of our subtle internal states. We often operate under ongoing levels of self-induced stress, which drips like corrosive poison into us daily. We prioritize the never-ending parade of things that we "must" do in the world at the expense of our self-care. This creates a false dichotomy between responsibilities and rest. We shortchange both by powering through tasks through sheer force of will.

All it takes to rebalance is to take a step back.

Listening to our emotions requires us to create the mental space for that to happen. We can only do this if we regularly turn down the mental noise, and hear the subtle communication coming into our awareness.

A fantastic way to do this is to regularly participate in intentional mindfulness practices.

Activities like meditation, tai chi, and yoga are backed by a growing scientifically backed list of health and wellness benefits. These ancient practices are an effective way to harness your whole being. All of them effectively calm and regulate the brain and nervous system—changing your responses to stress.

Incorporate mindfulness practices into your daily routine. These supportive activities then become habitual and more easily maintained. As they say in the airline passenger safety briefings: "Put your own oxygen mask on first before assisting others."

Don't shortchange your emotional self-care.

Avoid artificial addictions

As I covered earlier, brain chemicals have a powerful effect on our behaviors. They evolved to motivate us in the pursuit of survival goals. Our bodies naturally produce small quantities of these "happy" chemicals to get critical jobs accomplished. This flow quickly shuts off when it is not needed. Happiness is not a permanent state, but rather a source of short-term motivation.

We no longer live in small tribal bands. Our modern civilized society often creates distorted environments in which we chase the payoffs from the happy chemicals.

The abundance of sugary-fatty-salty processed foods is a perfect example. We evolved during a pre-agricultural time of food scarcity. High-sugar foods were a rare treat whose energy content was hoarded and stored as fat in the body. Processed carbohydrate foods that we consume have been specifically engineered to appeal to these evolutionary weaknesses. This has led to worldwide pandemics of obesity, heart disease, and diabetes.

Similarly, access to porn videos supports compulsive masturbation and the chemical payoff of an orgasm. Even in the absence of a willing sexual partner, we are free to conjure up any arousal scenario that we want.

Video games and virtual reality allow us to enter immersive worlds we can control. Inside of them we work hard to achieve goals and gain rewards. A continual stream of dopamine and adrenaline carefully crafted by the game designers keeps us motivated to take things, literally, to the next level.

These are all compulsive behaviors and many of them have proven difficult to manage or stop. But all of these activities at least release natural, body-produced neurotransmitters.

The real problem starts when we start eating, drinking, inhaling, or injecting substances from the outside. As you saw earlier in the book, synthetic drugs overpower the body's pleasure circuits—often leading to addiction. They also dampen our brain's response—so normal activities are no longer pleasurable in and of themselves.

Minimize or quit external drug use.

Don't be a loner

For mammals, life is a team sport. Isolation from our tribe or group usually means a quick death. But even among mammals, people have taken being social to a stunning extreme. We are the most social of all mammals by a wide margin. We are helpless at birth, reliant on others to learn to navigate the world around us.

We assume there is a world of social rules which operate at all times, even if we may not understand them yet. We have built-in critics who enforce our own and others' compliance with social norms and ideas.

Isolation makes us feel awful and will drive us mad. Despite amazing advances in transportation and communication, many people in our modern society live surrounded by strangers. We interact with them only in casual or superficial ways. We are living through a crisis of loneliness and despair despite being packed ever more tightly on the planet.

The effects of strong social support have been well documented. Lack of it can have disastrous consequences for our health, well-being, and longevity.

Being primal means being social. Find shared activities and groups to regularly participate in. It does not matter what the groups are. What matters is your regular interaction, and a certain level of connection and shared history.

Make sure you have ongoing social support.

Learn from others and teach something

We are social learners in a chain stretching back to prehistory. The need to transmit culture has evolved us into both curious students and willing teachers.

If you are interested in a certain subject, seek out someone to learn from in person. Often, this apprenticeship process is what is required to get you to the highest levels of knowledge in your chosen area of interest. By spending time with a skilled practitioner, you will pick up nuanced abilities. You can benefit from discernment which has taken many years or generations for others to acquire.

If you have achieved a measure of ability yourself, consider whether it is time to teach others. You will likely find the prestige payoff which you get from this will be quite substantial. Much personal and social goodwill stems from your role as a mentor, teacher, or a role model.

Learn it. Do it. Teach it.

Chapter 24

A PERSONAL CHALLENGE

Boom—technology is accelerating everything!

And the acceleration is itself accelerating. It is acting less like something predictable, and more like a rampaging tornado—transforming and violently reordering every aspect of existence on this planet. Daily life was essentially unchanged for many of our ancestors throughout their lifetimes, and even ensuing millennia. The same cannot be said of our age.

Feel the cadence of this buildup in your own body: fire, the wheel, printing presses, steam power, electricity, computers, and the rise of a worldwide network to instantly connect every person and sensor on the planet. Future shock is happening, and the next moment is already so yesterday…

Hurtling towards some adaptive, self-aware, fully autonomous global intelligence known as "the singularity," we are powerless to affect the course of our lives.

Quite unintentionally, these may be the very last days of regular humans. If we continue as a species at all, we will most likely be genetically engineered, and augmented to plug directly into this vast pulsing matrix. Ethical dilemmas around the very definition of what it means to be a person will shake many of our deeply cherished foundations. That is, if the machines decide to keep us around at all…

How do we live in the middle of turbulent changes, when there is less time for intentional thought?

What I have tried to give you in this book is a postcard from the past, and a snapshot of the present. It is my offering to help describe what the 8,000,000,000 of us on this planet share and have in common.

Our hypersocial natures are at the very heart of our being. We can accomplish great things in groups—wondrous leaps of imagination and common cause. Or, we can band together over trivial differences to subjugate and kill each other on an appalling scale.

To me the direction is clear. We must build the center. We need to pour our energy into community, while strong centripetal forces seek to pull us apart. This requires two conscious commitments.

Attach yourself to larger and larger tribes.

Concentric circles of self, family, neighborhood, city, state, nation, global humanity, all living things on the planet, and the universe are around us. If we attach to too small of a tribe, we turn everything and everyone else beyond its limit into a member of an outgroup. And we will aggressively struggle against them. Our tribe is safe, so screw everyone and everything else!

Be on the lookout for "leaders" who seek to divide and promise to champion your cherished cause ahead of the needs of others. Look instead for the universalists—those who struggle for basic human dignity and try to expand the circles of concern and right-action as widely as possible.

The flexibility to accept larger tribes is difficult. Much of our cultural learning happened during formative childhood years. Like anything else worthwhile, this deliberate expansiveness requires regular practice. Get comfortable being uncomfortable. A relentless commitment to seeing the perspective of different "others" will stretch and challenge you. But it will also open your heart and produce connection and understanding.

Strive to be greater than the sum of your parts.

Yes, we are irrational, and yes, we take evolutionary shortcuts that don't always serve us well. But we also have beautifully sophisticated emotions and intuitions. We are much more than a collection of tendencies and predispositions. Instead of cold clinical detachment and "rational" thought, we need to embrace our whole and complete selves. Through slowing down, and feeling deeply into the essence of things, we can truly unify the mind, body, and spirit. This is the best way to serve ourselves and all others.

"We call on the energies of the Within–the principle of wholeness, the energy and spirit of the mysterious. The color of this energy is gold. We welcome the gifts of balance, oneness, and the connection with all things, for all things are one and all things are related. The animal of the Within is the human being. The desire is for serenity and the emotion is of humility. We welcome the energies and spirit of Within. Aho!"

—Adapted lovingly from The Mankind Project's
"Welcoming-in of the directions" ceremony-**mkpusa.org**

Appendix
RECOMMENDED READING

I read the books below along with dozens of others, as well as countless articles and research papers, as part of writing my book. I hope that *Unleash Your Primal Brain* has whetted your appetite, and that you will want to explore some of the topics in more depth. I am sure that there are many other worthy books to explore, but the ones below should keep you excited and occupied for a while!

Look for these books and other resources at PrimalBrain.com, and info about Tim Ash at TimAsh.com.

100 Things Every Designer Needs To Know About People

Susan Weinschenk—ISBN-13: 978-0321767530

The focus is for the graphic designer and how to communicate information more effectively. But this handsome full-color book also covers dozens of behavioral and visual biases that have evolutionary origins. An updated 2nd edition is now available (ISBN-13: 978-0136746911).

Blink: The Power of Thinking Without Thinking

Malcolm Gladwell—ISBN-13: 978-0316010665

A testament to our unconscious brain, and its ability to synthesize massive amounts of information and turn them into near-instant decisions. Through vivid writing and compelling anecdotes, the power and limitations of the primitive brain are revealed.

Brainfluence: 100 Ways to Persuade and Convince Consumers with Neuromarketing

Roger Dooley—ISBN-13: 978-1118113363

The focus of this book is on neuromarketing and persuasion. But the compact chapters also cover a lot of the behavioral economics principles and perceptual biases that influence consumer choices.

Brain Rules: 12 Principles for Surviving and Thriving at Work, Home, and School

John Medina—ISBN-13: 978-0983263371

Snappy contemporary stories outline key parts of brain functioning for a non-technical audience. Applications to child development, learning, and memorization are explored. The importance of sleep and exercise are emphasized for brain performance.

The Business of Choice: Marketing to Consumers' Instincts

Matthew Willcox—ISBN-13: 978-0134772042

A solid overview and applications of behavioral science to marketing. Primarily written for professional marketers, but does touch on underlying evolutionary mechanisms and biases.

Buyology: Truth and Lies About Why We Buy

Martin Lindstrom—ISBN-13: 978-0385523899

An entertaining romp through the applications of brain imaging to advertising and marketing. Interesting insights into branding, tribal identity, and what influences buying decisions.

The Compass of Pleasure: How Our Brains Make Fatty Foods, Orgasm, Exercise, Marijuana, Generosity, Vodka, Learning, and Gambling Feel So Good

David Linden—ISBN-13: 978-0143120759

Written for a popular audience by a neuroscientist, this book breaks down the basic mechanisms of compulsion and pleasure seeking in the brain. The influence of neurochemistry on a wide variety of human behaviors and addictions is explored.

The Consuming Instinct: What Juicy Burgers, Ferraris, Pornography, and Gift Giving Reveal About Human Nature

Gad Saad—ASIN: B0084QW4MO

A vivid overview of our consumption habits, status seeking, and social and sexual signaling through the products we acquire.

Decoded: The Science Behind Why We Buy

Phil Barden—ISBN-13: 978-1118345603

This handsome full-color book not only looks good, but it is also packed with insights from an active marketing and branding practitioner about what makes consumers tick. It addresses how we perceive and take in information, the power of context, and ways that marketers can influence decisions.

Descartes' Error: Emotion, Reason, and the Human Brain

Antonio Damasio—ISBN-13: 978-0143036227

A dense book that explores the biological basis of thinking, emotion, and cognition. Detailed knowledge of brain anatomy and functional areas is either required or expected to be picked up as you read this book.

Groundswell: Winning in a World Transformed by Social Technologies

Charlene Li, Josh Bernoff—ISBN-13: 978-1422161982

A practical guide to engaging people, amplifying audiences, and creating brands in the age of social media.

Habits of a Happy Brain: Retrain Your Brain to Boost Your Serotonin, Dopamine, Oxytocin, & Endorphin Levels

Loretta Graziano Breuning—ISBN-13: 978-1440590504

A great overview of the motivational or "happy" chemicals that circulate in your brain, including their downsides.

How We Decide

Jonah Lehrer—ISBN-13: 978-0547247991

A punchy fly-by of decision-making strategies and learnings from diverse professional fields ranging from pilots, to athletes, and others who make high stakes decisions under pressure. It discusses the tradeoffs and handoffs between the intuitive brain and reasoning brain.

I, Mammal: How to Make Peace With the Animal Urge for Social Power

Loretta Graziano Breuning—ISBN-13: 978-1941959008

Explores the dynamics of social hierarchies among mammals. The focus is on how we react to both threats and opportunities to gain status in our tribal group.

Influence: The Psychology of Persuasion

Robert Cialdini—ISBN-13: 978-0061241895

An influential book based on direct marketing research that focuses primarily on the social nature of our decisions. It documents the effects of gift giving, public consistency with our commitments, the influence of our surrounding tribes and authority figures.

Landing Page Optimization: The Definitive Guide to Testing and Tuning for Conversions

Tim Ash, Rich Page, Maura Ginty—ISBN-13: 978-0470610121

The second edition of my bestselling book on Landing Page Optimization (written with brilliant co-authors). It is a detailed guide for the digital marketing professional on the art and science of Conversion Rate Optimization (CRO), and also covers quite a bit of information on the psychology of persuasion.

Nudge: Improving Decisions About Health, Wealth, and Happiness

Richard Thaler, Cass Sunstein—ISBN-13: 978-0143115267

Written by two eminent researchers, this book covers behavioral economics "nudges" to influence both personal and social decisions in a wide variety of applications.

Neuro Web Design: What Makes Them Click?

Susan Weinschenk—ISBN-13: 978-0321603609

A solid overview of applying psychological principles to the creation of websites.

Neuromarketing

Patrick Renvoisé, Christophe Morin—ISBN-13: 978-1595551351

A solid overview of the emerging field of neuromarketing. Covers approaches to engage the automatic response of the primitive brain regions.

Never Split the Difference: Negotiating As If Your Life Depended On It

Chris Voss, Tahl Raz—ISBN-13: 978-0062407801

A powerful book on negotiating in a high-stakes setting. Touches on many interpersonal and social dynamics that are key to getting the best possible outcome.

Pitch Anything: An Innovative Method for Presenting, Persuading, and Winning the Deal

Oren Klaff—ISBN-13: 978-0071752855

A dynamic first-person account of controlling the narrative in financial negotiations by understanding how to appeal to the primitive brain. Interesting perspective on the psychology of dominance and how to take others off of their game in a variety of situations.

Positioning: The Battle for Your Mind

Al Ries, Jack Trout—ISBN-13: 978-0071373586

A marketing classic that details how to frame the discussion of your product in the minds of the consumer and take advantage of subconscious shortcuts.

Predictably Irrational: The Hidden Forces That Shape Our Decisions

Dan Ariely—ISBN-13: 978-0061353246

A readable and thought-provoking first-hand account of a top behavioral economics researcher. Applications are mainly to consumer economics and forced choice decision making.

Sapiens: A Brief History of Humankind

Yuval Noah Harari—ISBN-13: 978-0062316097

A stunning tour-de-force of a book that charts a whirlwind course from man's early rise as a species through our cultural and social evolution to the present day.

Social: Why Our Brains Are Wired to Connect

Matthew Lieberman—ISBN-13: 978-0307889102

A compelling book about the basis of our social natures. Describes social versus non-social thinking as well as our need to continue to reexamine and update our social standing.

The Secret of Our Success: How Culture Is Driving Human Evolution, Domesticating Our Species, and Making Us Smarter

Joseph Henrich—ISBN-13: 978-0691178431

A compelling and powerful book that lays out the interdependence of our ability to transmit culture and our evolution. Numerous examples show the advantages of tribal learning over the abilities acquired by individuals through direct experience.

The Storytelling Animal: How Stories Make Us Human

Jonathan Gottschall—ISBN-13: 978-0544002340

Vividly describes why we need to create stories and explanations to make meaning out of our experiences. The power of the imagination and recurrence of universal themes are described from the perspective of psychology and evolution.

Thinking, Fast & Slow

Daniel Kahneman—ISBN-13: 978-0374533557

In this weighty tome, a career's worth of original research on psychology and decision making is distilled for the lay audience. Although a bit uneven at times, it can be repeatedly mined for a wide variety of purposes.

Why We Sleep: Unlocking the Power of Sleep and Dreams

Matthew Walker—ISBN-13: 978-1501144325

A comprehensive work by a top sleep researcher. Considers the evolution of sleep, disorders, impacts of sleep loss, and how to get better sleep. The most important self-help book I have read in many years.

Wired to Connect: The Surprising Link Between Brain Science and Strong, Healthy Relationships

Amy Banks—ISBN-13: 978-1101983218

The critical importance of our social natures is explored in this readable book. Practical strategies are also presented to strengthen our social and relationship abilities within the brain.

ABOUT THE AUTHOR

Tim Ash is an acknowledged authority on evolutionary psychology and digital marketing. He is a sought-after international keynote speaker, and the bestselling author of *Unleash Your Primal Brain* and *Landing Page Optimization* (with over 50,000 copies sold worldwide, and translated into six languages).

Tim has been mentioned by Forbes as a Top-10 Online Marketing Expert, and by Entrepreneur Magazine as an Online Marketing Influencer to Watch.

Tim is a highly-rated keynote speaker and presenter at over 200 events across four continents. He has been asked to return as a keynote at dozens of events because of the fantastic audience response. Tim shines on massive stages with over 12,000 attendees, as well as in intimate executive gatherings. He offers dynamic conference keynotes, workshops, and corporate training services (both in-person and virtually). Tim also selectively works as an online marketing advisor with senior executives.

For nineteen years he was the co-founder and CEO of SiteTuners—a strategic digital optimization agency. Tim has developed deep expertise in user-centered design, persuasion, understanding consumer behavior, neuromarketing, and landing page testing. In the mid-1990s he became one of the early pioneers in the discipline of website conversion rate optimization (CRO).

Tim has helped a number of major brands develop successful web marketing initiatives and created over $1,200,000,000 in value. Companies like Google, Expedia, eHarmony, Facebook, American Express, Canon, Nestle, Symantec, Intuit, Humana, Siemens, and Cisco have benefited from his deep understanding and innovative perspective.

He was the founding chair of the international Digital Growth Unleashed event series (with over 30 conferences in the US and Europe since 2010). Since 1995, he has authored more than 100 published articles. Tim was also the online voice of website improvement as the host of the Landing Page Optimization Podcast on WebmasterRadio.fm (over 130 recorded interview episodes with top online marketing experts).

Tim earned a dual-major Bachelor of Science degree "with highest distinction" in Computer Engineering and Cognitive Science from U.C. San Diego while studying on a U.C. Regents Scholarship (the highest academic award of the U.C. system). He stayed on at U.C. San Diego for Ph.D. studies focused on machine learning and artificial intelligence. Although Tim never defended his dissertation, he advanced to candidacy and also earned his Master's degree in Computer Science along the way.

Originally born in Russia, Tim has been a long-time resident of San Diego, where he lives with his wife and two children within walking distance of the Pacific Ocean. Tim was a conference-winning collegiate sabre fencer and Athlete of the Month at U.C. San Diego, and is a certified Tai Chi Chuan martial arts instructor. He is a poet, painter, and an avid photographer specializing in travel and fine-art figurative work.

MORE GOODNESS

Unlock Free Digital Bonuses
PrimalBrain.com/free (use code BKT1895)

Visit **PrimalBrain.com** for additional information about:

- This book and upcoming books in the Primal Brain series
- Additional resources and recommended reading
- Book club information
- Special branded editions of the book for your event or organization
- Contacting Tim regarding media interviews, podcasts, and book-related events

Visit **TimAsh.com** for additional information about:

- Having Tim keynote at your in-person or virtual event
- Getting an expert review of your website to improve its effectiveness
- Onsite or virtual digital marketing training for your team
- Development of a digital strategy for your company
- Online marketing advisory support for senior executives

Please review the book and spread the word to others!